KRISTIAN KLOECKL

# THE URBAN IMPROVISE

*Improvisation-Based Design for Hybrid Cities*

Yale

UNIVERSITY

PRESS

NEW HAVEN AND LONDON

Yale University Press books may be purchased in quantity for educational, business, or
promotional use. For information, please e-mail sales.press@yale.edu (U.S. office) or
sales@yaleup.co.uk (U.K. office).

Set in New Aster type by IDS Infotech Ltd., Chandigarh, India.
Printed in the United States of America.

ISBN 978-0-300-24304-8 (hardcover : alk. paper)
Library of Congress Control Number: 2019938092

A catalogue record for this book is available from the British Library.

This paper meets the requirements of ANSI/NISO Z39.48-1992 (Permanence of Paper).

10 9 8 7 6 5 4 3 2 1

*For Karim Alexander:*
*I hope that improvisation and the positions espoused in this*
*book will be helpful in your life.*

# CONTENTS

# ACKNOWLEDGMENTS

A book is the culmination of experiences, research, and conversations with numerous people over a long period of time. Some interactions are directly about the work; others seem unrelated at first, fleeting exchanges and observations that only later become clear in their relation to the book. I am tremendously grateful to all those who in many different ways have shown patience and generosity and contributed to the development of this book.

I am fortunate that I belong to a department and college that provide the space, encouragement, and support for developing a work such as this book. I am grateful for many inspiring conversations with my colleagues in the course of writing these pages, among whom Nathan Felde and Jane Amidon, in particular, have been mentors; Dietmar Offenhuber and Pedro Cruz are colleagues from my time at MIT and have provided inspiration through our conversations and through their rigorous and dedicated work; and Tad Hirsch encouraged me at the right times. Dan Adams and Ivan Rupnik have supported my work with our architecture students on issues of the urban improvise. Some of my students at Northeastern have worked with content in this book—their fresh and critical thinking inspires me every day.

An early conversation about improvisation with Antonio Ocampo-Guzman was key in my work that would become this book, as were conversations with Mark Lomanno about the field of critical improvisation. Conversations and project work with Jonathan Carr introduced me to Viewpoints improvisation, which became foundational for my work in this book. The collaboration with him, Mark Sivak, and Camden Phalen provided an early opportunity to implement some of the concepts from this book in a public installation.

The 2025 Dean's Fellowship of the College of Arts, Media, and Design supported my work on this book, and I am grateful for an enthusiastic and brilliant group of students that worked with me in exploring all those improvisational instances in the daily life of a hybrid city. These include Noah Appleby, Fiona Galey, Julia Janigian, Alyssa Kurien, and Win Overholser—and a special thank-you to Jeffrey Weng for his collaboration.

I am grateful to Carlo Ratti, who invited me in 2006 to join the then-nascent Senseable City Lab at MIT, where we carried out some of the early work on cities and networked technologies. Over the course of the following seven years and while heading the lab's Real Time City Group and building up the Singapore-based research team, I had the chance to engage with numerous people from a diverse range of backgrounds that provided a fruitful context for conversations and interactions that helped form my ideas on the nexus of design, cities, and technology. Among them, I am particularly grateful to Clio Andris, Eric Baczuk, Assaf Biderman, Rex Britter, Francesco Calabrese, Xiaoji Chen, Jennifer Dunnam, Fabien Girardin, Daniel Gutierrez, E. Roon Kang, Aaron Koblin, David Lee, Diego Maniloff, Vincenzo Manzoni, Till Nagel, Christine Outram, Bernd Resch, Francisca Rojas, Oliver Senn, Andres Sevtsuk, Aaron Siegel, Christian Sommer, Andrea Vaccari, and Anthony Vanky.

I am grateful for a number of formative conversations with the late William Mitchell about what he already then saw as some of the critical challenges and threats looming over the work with personal data and cities. Hugh Dubberly and Paul Pangaro continue to be treasured resources on systems, cybernetics, and conversations. Bryan Shiles inspired conversations during an eventful, fun, and rewarding collaboration on workplace and public realm.

Daniel Cardoso Llach and Terry Knight provided helpful and constructive early feedback on parts of the manuscript. Mark Shepard provided encouraging conversations and support since we first met while I led the Trash Track project installed at the Sentient City exhibition he curated at the Architectural League of New York. I thank Jordan Geiger for the opportunity to engage with another designer captured by the performative, and Omar Khan for inspiring discussions in Buffalo.

I thank Mike Phillips for conversations on interactivity, design, cooking, and moving walls at a tiny Greek restaurant in Athens at the end of the Hybrid City conference and Raoul Bunschoten and Liss Werner for hosting me in Berlin for the Cybernetics: State of the Art conference, where I presented some of my early work on what would later become this book.

I thank Bradley Cantrell for conversations about wildness and wilderness in design; Paul Dourish for an encouraging early conversation in Boston about the central ideas of the book; and Adam Greenfield for an inspiring conversation at MIT about hooks to connect things differently, before the publication of his book on "everyware."

Brenda Laurel's work on computers as theater has been one of the key inspirations for developing the work in this book. Giovanni Anceschi's work on design as *registica*, theory of staging, has provided an early glimpse into performative notions of design; he has been an inspiring teacher first and then a colleague at IUAV. Medardo Chiapponi, back in Milan and Venice, was my teacher, dissertation adviser, and then colleague and mentor as I moved from work in industry to the world of academia and research.

I thank Billie Jo Joy for her generosity in introducing me to the practice of improvisation in the work with her improvisation group. I feel an enormous sense of gratitude toward Sensei Davide Rizzo, who has given me much through the practice of karate at the dojo in Venice for several years, oss! His kind, impassioned— and painful—introduction to the martial arts has provided me with a deep understanding of how, just as in improvisation, repetition and novelty are two sides of the same coin.

The collaboration with a publisher on a book is as much a professional contract as it is a personal encounter with an editor. I have been fortunate to collaborate on this book with Joe Calamia at Yale University Press, who with incredible kindness, patience, and support has guided this book project from an early idea to the finished book you now hold in your hands.

Last but not least, I feel a deep sense of gratitude toward my wife for her loving patience and support throughout all stages of developing this book and toward my son for his love and laughter, which always help clarify priorities in life.

THE URBAN IMPROVISE

# 1 INTRODUCTION

It also happens that, if you move along Marozia's compact walls, when you least expect it, you see a crack open and a different city appears. Then, an instant later, it has already vanished. Perhaps everything lies in knowing what words to speak, what actions to perform, and in what order and rhythm; or else someone's gaze, answer, gesture is enough; it is enough for someone to do something for the sheer pleasure of doing it, and for his pleasure to become the pleasure of others: at that moment, all spaces change, all heights, distances; the city is transfigured, becomes crystalline, transparent as a dragonfly. But everything must happen as if by chance, without attaching too much importance to it, without insisting that you are performing a decisive operation.

—ITALO CALVINO, *Invisible Cities*

## A DAY IN THE LIFE . . .

A man steps out into a cold winter morning. His eyes are fixed on his watch, while his other hand clenches his bag, grabbed as he rushed out the door.

It is 1992. The man is running late for an early work meeting. To catch the 6:35 a.m. bus, he will have to make it to the bus stop in five minutes instead of the usual seven. The winter bus schedule has kicked in; he consulted the printed schedule at the bus stop the day before to find out the right departure time to make it in for his meeting. He hastily rushes through the morning snowstorm, but as he turns around the last corner he sees the taillights of his bus as it pulls away from the stop. He missed it. He glances at his wristwatch in disbelief. One minute early! How was that possible with all that snow? Or was it the earlier bus that ran a massive delay? Frustrated, he reaches the bus stop to check how long he will need to wait for the next bus. Twenty minutes! Not a good way to start the day.

Now, fast-forward to 2020. A woman wakes up in an apartment in an unfamiliar city. She planned her trip at the last minute, and she found the apartment on Airbnb's room-sharing platform. The mobility app Transit informs her that the nearest subway line is running a delay due to a worker strike. The app recommends that she walk an extra fifteen minutes and take a bus to reach the destination of her appointment on time. She hadn't planned a walk, but she decides to take the advice.

As she steps out of the building, she spots a yellow ofo bike just a bit farther down the road. She had signed up with that dockless bike-sharing service a few weeks ago and is pleasantly surprised to see the bikes in this city too.

As she heads to unlock the bike with her smartphone, the phone vibrates before switching off—no more power. Now she remembers that there was no charger in her apartment. No more unlocking the bike, no more directions to the bus stop, and, most concerning, no address for her meeting. What was the person's name again that she was about to meet? The woman scrambles in her pocket for a while and finds her external battery pack. Phew . . .

After a couple minutes of recharging, her phone starts up again. A scan of the bike's code from the ofo app, and she pedals off to the bus stop. Her phone keeps her informed about the projected time of arrival of her bus at the stop, taking into account actual traffic conditions. In fact, her Transit app now, after all the time spent reanimating her phone, recommends yet another route, but the woman, now keen on a bike ride, continues, ignoring the app's recommendation.

Bus departure times are not scheduled in this city. Instead, they are determined on the basis of real-time travel demand and are adjusted continuously. The woman reaches the bus stop just before the bus turns around the corner. She parks her bike, closes the lock to complete the trip on the bike-sharing platform, and boards the bus, also paying with her smartphone. As she rides the bus, the driver informs passengers that the bus will run the following three stops express, skipping the stops on the basis of real-time passenger demand data. One passenger gets off at the following stop to take the next nonexpress bus to one of the stops that will be skipped. He seemed annoyed.

The remaining passengers are satisfied with a quicker connection. The woman is a few stops away from her destination as she receives an update on her phone that informs her about the subway line now running again and that she could reach her destination a few minutes earlier by switching to the subway line at the next stop—despite the bus running express. She, however, is enjoying the bus ride, learning about this new city. Screens inside the bus provide information about places they pass by as she crosses the city. She just found out about a small music store that she had heard about and that she now knows how to get to. She makes a mental note to stop by later in the day. Along the ride she checks her email and responds to some messages for work, arriving at the location of her appointment with plenty of time.

These are two different scenarios of the mundane act of moving through urban space using public transportation a quarter century apart. Are these scenarios realistic? Pretty much. Are they exaggerated? Certainly. There is a tendency for a positivist idealism in scenarios that involve digital technologies in general and those in the context of cities in particular. While I have tried to introduce some nuance, exaggerating some elements helps to leverage the scenarios to make an argument.

The first scenario deals with a printed schedule as the mediating interface between the traveler and the transport system. This interface is fixed, constructed prior to the event of actual rides, on the basis of historical statistical probabilities, and it is blind toward how activities actually play out. Passenger and bus will only successfully meet if their actual behavior complies with the plan devised when the schedule was constructed—that is, if both bus and passenger manage to meet at the agreed time and location.

The static tool of a printed schedule cannot take into account how the continuously changing traffic situation impacts the ride duration between bus stops. It cannot adjust to how many people will actually board and alight at each stop, requiring more or less time. It cannot take into account the speed at which this operation will happen on the basis of travelers' ages, physical conditions, or other circumstances. It cannot take into account potential technical complications of a bus that requires a checkup, a repair, or the use of a substitute bus.

This first scenario is an example of an urban interaction that is *deaf* and *mute* to how things actually work during the activity or how they work differently in any given situation. It does not consider that plans can be made but can rarely be followed without adjustment to the incidental, the circumstantial, the contingent.[1]

The situation in today's scenario appears similar at first but is remarkably different in important ways. The woman still uses public transportation to move across town. Subway and bus are still as popular or unpopular as they had been, depending on the city and the sociocultural context considered. Where things begin to differ, however, is the way in which urban operations interface with the actual context and situation and how these are made intelligible to different participant groups at the time of possible action. The exchange of information between bus and prospective passenger helps facilitate their encounter at a time and place that works for both. The information that facilitates this encounter is updated in real time. At any given time, the prospective bus passenger can *see* the location of the bus in relation to the bus stop (or the time required to arrive there on the basis of an estimate). The behavior of the bus, in this way, is *virtually visible* to the traveler.[2] By monitoring boarding and alighting passengers through the electronic ticketing system, the bus *knows* at any time its occupancy and free capacity—the number of passengers aboard and available seats. Boarding and alighting information is used to pick up on rising demand patterns for connections between any two specific stops of the bus line.[3] This information is used to dynamically add or reduce the number of buses along a line or to send buses *express*.

The buses of a responsive transport system, as the one described, adapt their behavior to the actual situation, and so do passengers. Both impact each other; both *listen* to each other. They condition each other without any one controlling the other as such.

The dockless bike-sharing system that emerged around 2015 has further increased the flexibility of mobility options in cities. Without requiring any fixed and physical docking stations, the operation of these bikes relies on bike-based GPS, cellular, QR code, and Bluetooth technologies. A smartphone app unlocks the bike in a few seconds, bikes can be parked (and found) anywhere in the city, and trips can start and end at any location without any prior commitment. (The dockless bike-sharing system is discussed in more detail in chapter 6 of this book.)

Urban systems (related to mobility or otherwise) that support interactions of this kind represent a shift from a predominantly plan-based way of operating to one that is dynamic and responsive and that adapts to a continuously changing context. It displays a behavior that engages with human participants. Activity is detected and interpreted, actions are modulated, and behavior is adapted in response to unpredictable situations in feedback loops and in a continuous give-and-take.

This kind of responsive behavior resembles that of performers in an improvised music, dance, or theater performance. In both, interactions are not based on a plan; action and feedback are tightly coupled through feedback loops involving sensing and attention. Behavior is conceived and executed in the moment, allowing for unplanned overall behavior to emerge.

And this is precisely the core of this book's exploration: how to use insights from the practice and study of performance improvisation to inform the design of interactive artifacts, systems, and environments in the context of today's networked cities.

I argue that technology-mediated interactions in cities today can be better understood and conceived of by adopting an improvisation-based design perspective. This allows us to better disclose the potential of today's technology-saturated urban environments for urban dwellers.

Improvisation is here examined as a *framework for making*, for the design of interactions in what I refer to as the *hybrid city*. I leverage the essence of improvisation as an art, a practice, and a concept to construct a system of ideas to help better understand the current condition of the hybrid city. And to facilitate the design of urban interventions, I put forth a set of four principles, or positions, that underlie the design of interactions in hybrid cities.

## DESCRIBING CITIES

Over the past two decades, the nature of the built urban environment has changed in significant ways. Vast networks of mobile and embedded digital devices have become ubiquitous in the physical urban fabric. The pervasiveness of connected devices has transformed the built environment into spaces and objects that have a more fluid behavior.[4] These objects and environments are capable of sensing, computing, and acting in real time. They can change their behavior in response to their own system state, histories of past actions and interactions, the behavior of humans and machines within their reach, and environmental conditions.

In scales from the spoon to the city, objects and systems have become entangled with information technologies that exchange information in real time. Today, architects, designers, developers, and other stakeholders are engaged not only in defining form and function but also in constructing the *behavior* and *etiquette* of responsive objects and environments as they perform together with people in the complex context of the city.

Feedback loops are a key component in the tight integration of networked information technologies in our built environment. Sensors and other computational devices in urban environments are wirelessly networked, and information exchange happens in real time. Think of your mobile phone or your smart watch. Both contain a large number of sensors and are constantly connected to remote servers through multiple network technologies (cellular, Wi-Fi, Bluetooth, etc.). Think of proximity sensors employed to help you park your car, open automatic doors, and turn on the lights as you approach. Sensors in the wastewater stream provide information about the substances emitted by urban systems, and air-quality sensors monitor concentrations of pollutants in the air. Subway stations can narrow the entrance passage in the case of excessive passenger pressure to ensure safety on the platform, and traffic lights operate using algorithms that take into account the traffic conditions monitored in proximity by cameras and induction loops under the road. Aggregate cellphone-network data is used to evaluate traffic conditions, rerouting drivers dynamically; airports use Bluetooth-device counters for queue management; office rooms pick up on carbon dioxide concentrations to calibrate the air-conditioning operation in response to the number of people present at any given time.

Urban systems that support interactions of this kind are *performative* in their nature. Going beyond simple action-reaction couplings, they become truly interactive.[5] They adapt their response to the contingencies of situations as they detect and interpret activities of which they are an integral part.

I look at improvisation not as doing something in a makeshift manner but instead as a process characterized by a simultaneity of conception and action, in which iterative and recursive operations lead to the emergence of dynamic structures that continue to feed into the action itself. An improvisation-based perspective is a compelling way to better understand and frame the design of interactions in the context of today's technology-imbued cities.

## BEYOND THE SMART CITY

When talking about networked information technologies in an urban context, it is difficult not to address the *smart city*, a term and concept that has gained significant notoriety. Before the *smarts* were declared for cities, we had *smart technologies* and *smart materials*. Developed in the 1980s, smart materials have qualities that change in response to environmental conditions such as light, pressure, or temperature—for example, shape-memory alloys that can be bent and return to their original shape when exposed to heat. In a similar way, *smart technologies* describe technology systems that display a similar kind of response that is context dependent and uses sensors, computational devices, and actuators. The *smart* label works when attributed to engineering systems that overcome rigid plans of operation but runs into trouble when applied to a complex and multifaceted entity that, more than only material and technological components, involves social, institutional, economic, historical, cultural, and other aspects.

There is a plethora of different smart city definitions, but a common element in all is the widespread deployment of mobile and embedded networked information and communication technologies that are integrated in the physical fabric of the city.[6] The declared objective of this ideal of interconnectivity is to support urban operations and planning for an increase in efficiency of services to improve the social, economic, and environmental well-being of citizens.[7] What the terms of such efficiency are is indeed one of the controversies in the critical debate about the smart city.

Confident claims associated with this position point toward efficiency in terms of zero energy wastage, no traffic jams, no air and water pollution, and zero crime-threatening inhabitants. IBM in one of its "Smarter Planet" ads suggests systems would "reduce traffic by 20%," "preventing crime before it happens," and promises "smarter public safety for a smarter planet."[8] Living PlanIT claims that "a complete picture of building state, usage, and operations is continually maintained, allowing constant optimization of energy, resources, environment and occupant support and convenience systems." Germany-based Siemens instead looks ahead, claiming that "several decades from now, cities will have countless autonomous, intelligently functioning IT systems that will have perfect knowledge of users' habits and energy consumption, and provide optimum service."[9]

The concept of the smart city is not without criticism, however. It is criticized for being technocentric and sympathetic to approaches of "total control," as manifest in the installation of urban control centers.[10] An example is Rio de Janeiro's Operations Center, installed by IBM in December 2010. It brings together data streams from a range of urban systems that become visible to operators of technology systems and city administrations but remain invisible to citizens.[11] This focus on notions of centralized control in the smart city concept undermines the idea of a city as a complex social and spatial entity where structures emerge through citizens' collective activity.

Another critique is that the smart city ignores the diversity of sociocultural contexts and outsources governance to corporations. The critique also points to a one-solution-fits-all approach that relies on information technologies and a predominant reference to the formats of Western industrialized cities. This conflicts with the real diversity of urban conditions that exist in different parts of the world as well as even within any one city itself.[12] The smart city concept, true to its technology-based origin, has come to view the deployment of technology in cities as progressive per se and is critiqued for the application of predictive profiling and for a depiction of the use of algorithms and analytics as objective and void of ideology.[13]

The smart city concept in this way has come to recall the modernist thinking of the early twentieth century. Then, traditional forms of human practice (architecture, social organization, urban forms, everyday activities of daily life) were considered obsolete and unfit for the newly developing socioeconomic context of the industrialized world. To make it *new* became the imperative to heal the troubles of human existence in the modernist era; to make it *smart* would seem to be its equivalent today.

As a response to this technocentric mind-set of the smart city concept, a more substantial consideration of human and social aspects in the development of urban technologies has recently moved the focus from *smart city* to *smart citizen*.[14] Social dynamics and the human component have here moved center stage in working with urban information technologies and aspire to respond more directly to the needs, dreams, and aspirations of citizens.[15]

As part of this changed perspective, participatory forms of design have taken ground in the context of networked technologies in urban environments. These forms of design go beyond a simplistic problem-solution coupling that has its origin in an inherent limitation in the underlying human-centered design approach. Calls for an integration of perspectives of participatory design and speculative design approaches point to notions of nonanthropocentric design. This perspective is based on a conceptual *decentering of the human* as well as on new forms of citizenship and cohabitation to address sociotechnical complexity such as economic and ecological crisis in more responsible, accountable, and ethical ways when working with emerging technologies.[16]

Citizen participation is seen as a key to a more critical way of working with networked urban technologies, yet forms of participation vary considerably. In some instances, the focus is on compliance with expected behaviors that are identified as desirable, including strategies of nudging or incentive-based systems.[17] Another form of participation regards citizens as a source of information provided through smartphone apps or other digital interfaces. Citizen participation in the form of direct involvement in the planning and management processes, instead, involves residents more comprehensively and taps into informal networks of knowledge, on the one hand, creating a sense of ownership, on the other.[18]

Different modes of designing interventions that integrate networked information technologies directly impact constitutional practices of city making. They change the experience citizens have of their cities, but, even more, they change the nature of the subject, of what it means to be a citizen and what it means to have agency. They condition the modes of urban politics and reshape the foundations of the democratic way we live together in cities.[19]

The term *smart city* has revealed itself as inadequate for a more critical and pluralistic discourse about the intertwining of networked information technologies and cities. Urban dwellers today are engaging with both their physical environment and digital technologies simultaneously. Cities are becoming hybrids of material and information in a way never seen before. They are becoming what I refer to in this book as *hybrid cities*, which tightly integrate digital information technologies within the built environment and across a broad range of domains. This hybridification manifests itself in different ways in different cities around the world and within any one city itself. When I refer to *the hybrid city* as a singular, I talk about this emergent condition rather than any one specific city as such.

I suggest using the term *hybrid city*, which originates from the Hybrid City conference series that started in 2011 in Athens,[20] as a humbler and more agnostic term that does not claim any particular achievements or betterments from the technology per se but that is limited to describing the digital-physical hybridification of urban environments. This leaves room to discuss implications of this condition with more nuance and with distinction in regard to particular instances. It leaves room to bring the focus on *how* to work with technologies in hybrid cities and what frameworks of human-technology interaction are fit to analyze and synthesize, or create, the hybrid city.

## MODELS OF INTERACTION

The pervasive integration of networked information technologies in the built urban environment poses a challenge to extant frameworks and models of human-machine interaction, which over the years have been the basis for how we understand and design interactive artifacts and systems.

The *interface* is perhaps one of the most successful conceptual models with which to contemplate human-product interactions. While the term is today commonly used to describe the visual appearance of digital screens, the framework is more comprehensive and also refers to interactions with nondigital artifacts.[21] In general, interface describes an entity that stands *in between* (inter-), at a point where two or more systems meet and interact. It is a sur*face* that is presented to the view of someone or something. This surface presents to the one system something meaningful about the other system; it *represents* the one system to the other system. Interface is a particularly effective conceptual model when configurations of human-technology interactions are fixed, such as in the case of physical interfaces using sliders, levers, dials, handles, and so on.

The plasticity of the nature of human-computer interfaces has led to the development of alternative models for conceptualizing interaction, and the model that I present in this book builds on these models. The notion of *conversation* as a model for interaction dates back to the 1970s, when Gordon Pask generated his work on conversation theory.[22] It has been used and discussed extensively since then (by Ranulph Glanville and Hugh Dubberly, among others) and has recently garnered renewed attention in the form of the so-called *conversational interfaces*.[23] The notion of *common ground* as a framework for human-computer interaction (HCI) comes from Herbert Clark's work in communication theory in the 1990s.[24] Both these notions suggest models in which meaning is negotiated and co-created between humans and computers as part of the interactions. In this sense, interface is no longer a simple notion by which humans and computers represent themselves to one another. Rather, it forms a shared context for action in which both are agents in an Aristotelian sense.[25]

This shift of focus to *activity* has been enhanced by the growing integration of computational devices into many facets of everyday life. Through the work of the anthropologist Lucy Suchman, the focus has shifted to action as contingent on *context* and *situation* and, relatedly, to *embodied action* and the mutual constitution of subject and object as part of *activity* as the unit of investigation.[26]

Brenda Laurel's model of *interface as theater*, first published in 1991, was updated in 2014; Don Norman states in the foreword to the latter edition that "the first edition was ahead of its time. This new edition comes at just the right time. Now the world is ready."[27] Theater is presented as a model for the performance of intentional activity in which both human and computer have a role, concerned with representing whole actions that involve multiple agents.[28]

Although this conceptual model opens up fascinating new ground, it refers essentially to scripted theater. However, in scripted theater, unlike real life, the process of choice and decision-making takes place during script writing and rehearsal, before the actual staging of the performance. Conception and presentation occur in sequence and at distinct moments in time. In the sense that drama formulates the enactment and not the action, it is unlike real life.

Instead, in improvisational performances, as in real life, anything can happen. Actions are situated in a unique context that is always in flux, and the focus is on dynamic choice in a dynamic environment.

By identifying the interactions in and with urban responsive environments and the art of improvisation as fundamentally related topics of investigation, we can identify a set of underlying positions that point toward a foundational model for urban interaction design. I suggest that this can provide a framework by which today's interactive urban systems might be more systematically understood.

## IMPROVISATION AND THE CITY

Improvisation and the city have been intertwined throughout history. A prominent historical tie is that of the *commedia dell'arte* performances that date back to the sixteenth century in cities of the Italian peninsula. Commedia dell'arte was the first professional form of actor groups—a traveling business enterprise—focused on improvisation. On the basis of a schema or *scenario*, actors would do away with a script and improvise their performances for a number of reasons: improvisation allowed the performance to be adapted to the many local languages and dialects of the peninsula; the story could be adapted up to the last minute to embrace current local events and the political situation; and by not being limited to written scripts, performers were not prone to political censorship.[29]

The subversive nature of acting-in-the-moment is also what Michel de Certeau describes in *The Practice of Everyday Life*, when he focuses on the innumerable "ways of operating," the everyday tactics, by means of which users reappropriate space organized by powerful strategies and techniques of sociocultural production. De Certeau investigates how people take shortcuts between formal paths; what people actually do with systems put in place for them to consume; and what clandestine forms of practices and procedures of everyday interactions exist relative to structures of expectation, negotiation, and improvisation.[30]

Today, the city is frequently described as an entity that functions akin to a computer—"the city itself is turning into a constellation of computers"[31]—numerically controlled and on a binary basis. However, this image somehow does not resemble the motives behind people's choice to move to cities in the first place. Enrico Moretti in "The New Geography of Jobs" describes how people move to what are essentially idea factories: cities full of people.[32] People move to cities for something that exceeds their expectation—a search for the *unexpected* and for the *unforeseen*.

## WHAT KIND OF IMPROVISATION

This consideration points to the very essence of the term *improvisation*: its Latin root, *proviso*, indicates a condition attached to an agreement, a stipulation made beforehand. With the prefix *im-*, *improvisation* indicates that which has not been agreed on or planned and thus presents itself as unforeseen and unexpected. However, improvisation is a process that is often misunderstood. A common interpretation is that when something is improvised, it is to make up for the lack of something or to get by in some way until the plan that was lost can be recovered.[33] The view of improvisation that I adopt goes beyond this interpretation.

In the context of music, improvisation refers to a playing in the moment or a composing in the flow. It is a process characterized by a simultaneity of both conception and presentation; and during the act of execution, the situation at hand continues to feed into what is being played.[34] To talk about improvisation also means to consider the notion of inventiveness, involving elements both of novelty and of repetition of past patterns. We can "conceive of improvisation as an iterative and recursively operating process where dynamic structures emerge from the processing and reprocessing of elements."[35] With this understanding, we capture more of the essence of the practice, which enables us to identify structures in a process that can at first appear ephemeral.

We typically underestimate the investment in attention, study, and practice that is the foundation for every improvised performance. Requiring a heightened awareness both of self and of others, an improvisation is based, to a critical extent, on the performer's past practice and experience. When performers improvise, they elaborate on existing material in relation to the unforeseen ideas that emerge out of the context and the unique conditions of the performance. In this way, variations are created and new features are added every time, making performances distinct.[36] Improvisation overcomes several dichotomies instilled by modern thought. Its practice overcomes clear distinctions between repetition and novelty, discipline and spontaneity, security and risk, individual and group, and, ultimately, order and disorder. It does so by doing away with a binary opposition and embracing a mind frame of complexity, in which order and disorder—information and noise—form a mutually constitutive relationship.[37]

In improvisation many actions do not receive their full meaning until after the act has occurred. What one performer does will redefine the meaning of the previous action of another performer, which again will be conditioned by the following action. These recursive processes define themselves because their definition cannot be attributed to the intention of a single actor or even all participating actors. In systems theory, emergence describes the appearance of something new that could not be anticipated but that was born out of the interaction between previously present elements.[38] Adapting a systems view of improvisation makes the tension between the notions of stability and variation a productive one.

## A NEW ROLE FOR IMPROVISATION IN DESIGN

Equipped with this perspective on the nature of improvisation, in this book I identify four key positions that are recurrent in different types of improvisation and that I propose to consider as foundational elements for an improvisation-based model of urban interaction design. These are elaborated in greater detail in chapter 5.

*Open beginnings: Design for initiative ensures openness.* A critical aspect of improvisational performance involves the beginnings—and, as such, the notions of agency and autonomy of a person or system.

*Timing and agency: Awareness of time ensures the relevance of actions.* Time and timing are key in improvisation. Planning and action collapse into a single moment, and the configuration of content in time and space molds the meaning of action.

*Understanding in action: Forms of action are understood in the making.* In ensemble work, each performer feeds off and builds on what others do. As they interact with each other, performers pass cues back and forth, consciously or unconsciously, and these cues are perceived and interpreted. They become part of a collective creation of meaning that informs the interaction.

*Unexpected interactions: Interactions themselves are other than expected.* In the unplanned and in-the-moment nature of improvisation, it deals with the unexpected and the uncontrollable—that which cannot be fully known and that is *other* from what we know. Folding the rich art and practice of improvisation into the way we look at the design of interactions in today's hybrid urban environments means allowing for this otherness in the way we shape and activate our environment.

### THE HYBRID CITY HAS BEGUN TO IMPROVISE

Artifacts and environments that display some of these four characteristics of improvisational dynamics already exist. The following examples represent instances of a trajectory toward an improvisational perspective on the design of urban interactions. These examples will be examined, along with two other cases, in more detail in chapter 6.

One example is Slothbots, a project by Plymouth University's research lab i-DAT, which consists of large autonomous and box-like robots that move very slowly, at a speed that is barely perceptible. By doing so, they reconfigure the physical architecture over time as a result of their interactions with people. Slothbots pick up on the use of the space they are in and how it changes throughout the day, and they reposition themselves in response to and anticipation of new interactions with building occupants.[39]

With respect to the key positions I propose for an improvisation-based model for interaction, the spatial configurations generated by the Slothbots are characterized by an openness that is continuously renegotiated between the responsive physical element and the human constituents of the space as they condition and reflect each other's behavior. The where, when, and how of the Slothbots' moves emerge out of the interaction with building residents and the physical context. The moves involve no plan, as such, but rather a protocol of constraints that together with people's behavior results in the movement being constantly conceived as it is enacted. The object cannot be controlled and might block passage, divide space, direct or facilitate flow, or do otherwise. These meanings are attributed as they emerge from the interplay between people and the Slothbots, rather than being prescribed. The effect of this ongoing process of regeneration is remarkable because it results in a continuous novelty, bestowed on a space that might otherwise seem familiar.

Another example is dockless bike-sharing systems. Today's latest generation of bike-sharing systems does away with docking stations and consists of networked bikes alone. Equipped with a lock that integrates GPS location monitoring and cellular data transmission functionalities, these bikes are physically scattered throughout the urban territory without fixed locations while remaining connected to a remote sensing platform. Users unlock a bike in seconds, for a fixed price, and can park the bike in any location.[40]

These dockless bike-sharing systems are characterized by a high degree of openness and invite people to take initiative due to the immediacy of spotting one, unlocking it, and pedaling away. The bike in its physicality has become the interface to the digital system that mediates the service. Its openness lies in the enormous room for individual appropriation of the service within one's everyday practice. Awareness of time ensures the relevance of actions in that the choice of starting a ride does not require a decision about its destination, as is the case with dock-based bike-sharing systems. The system integrates into urbanites' activities in an ad hoc modality. Forms of action are understood in the making in that the bike system is being reconfigured continuously by where people ride and park the bikes. Concentration and sprawl are entangled with the purpose attributed by urban residents, ensuring intrinsically that the system remains relevant to a city as it evolves. Unexpected interactions are an integral part of this system, which cannot as such be meaningfully predicted. A bike can be parked right outside your door, offering you a ride, as described in the scenario in the beginning of this chapter. It does not matter to you what the probability is for this to happen; it matters only when it actually happens. The otherness of the system is also found in the manifold uses and abuses of the system, the boundaries for the latter being negotiated through every single concrete act.

## IMPROVISATION PRACTICE FOR DESIGN

The discussion of the preceding examples is a preview of how the proposed key positions of an improvisation-based model can be employed to analyze existing projects. The rich variety of methods and techniques that improvisation performers use in their training and practice provides a further resource to instrumentalize this model within the design process. Several of these are well articulated and documented. Performers use these techniques to prepare and hone their ability to improvise in the moment of performance. I propose to look at these techniques as a resource to inform the design of responsive systems and environments.

The improvisation technique Viewpoints is particularly relevant to the scope of this book. It was developed in the 1970s by the choreographer Mary Overlie, was later formalized by the theater director Anne Bogart and the playwright Tina Landau, and is used extensively today.

In Viewpoints improvisation, individual and collective activity emerges in real time on the basis of actors' heightened awareness and immediate response to any of nine viewpoints that form the structural basis of the technique and that are temporal or spatial in nature: tempo, duration, kinesthetic response, and repetition are the temporal viewpoints; spatial relationship, topography, shape, gesture, and architecture are the spatial viewpoints.[41] The challenge in improvisation is always *what to do*, as there is no plan or script, and these viewpoints help actors to focus their attention on specific aspects in the development of their improvisation.

In improvisational practice, these viewpoints are first introduced one at a time, guiding actors' awareness, attention, and action. Then, multiple viewpoints are combined, developing complex dynamics of interaction. A Viewpoints coach can facilitate the process and guide the actors' awareness to any one or any combination of viewpoints in their work.[42]

Chapter 7 of this book provides a detailed discussion of how improvisation techniques can be employed in the design process. Using the example of Viewpoints, each of the nine viewpoints that performers use to dynamically engage with their environment can become a constitutive reference for the articulation of the behavior of designed interactions in hybrid city environments. In this way, techniques for the practice and training of improvisation performance can become part of a framework for the design of interactions that is less prescriptive and instead provides an open context for citizens to engage with.

## PLACES MADE OVER TO IMPROVISATION

"The worth of cities is determined by the number of places in them made over to improvisation," notes Siegfried Kracauer in *Straßen in Berlin und anderswo*.[43] Graeme Gilloch in "Seen from the Window: Rhythm, Improvisation and the City" synthesizes this pledge emphatically in his thesis for a future city: "for moments, against monuments."[44]

This book contextualizes, proposes, and experiments with a new model for interactions with responsive artifacts and environments in today's hybrid cities. Design has so far looked at improvisation for the enactment of user scenarios and personas to identify opportunities and challenges of design interventions. The art and practice of improvisation and the emerging field of critical improvisation studies, in conjunction with the development of networked and responsive information technologies, instead provides an opportunity to bring a more foundational perspective of improvisation into the design domain.

The following chapters explore how a focus on improvisational performance can expand on earlier and alternative models of interaction used in the field of design. It describes the tight relation between improvisation and the urban dimension, and it examines how a detailed look at the nature of improvisation as a system enables us to formulate a number of key positions that point toward an improvisation-based model for interaction. The analysis of existing projects illustrates how elements of an improvisation-based perspective on interaction are already being used in the field and how they relate to key positions of an improvisation-based model.

Finally, this book illustrates, through a specific application example, how improvisation techniques can be used to directly guide the design of responsive urban environments. Design, in this perspective, moves the behavior and the performance of things center stage, taking inspiration from nonscripted forms of interaction and embracing the unforeseen and unexpected as constructive aspects of its production.

## CHAPTER OVERVIEW AND HOW TO USE THIS BOOK

Following this introduction, the book is articulated in six chapters and concludes with an epilogue. The chapters are best read in sequence; but as the argument of the book suggests, unexpected connections will emerge, and I invite the reader to follow along individual and unique paths through the pages as they unfold.

Chapter 2, "When the City Begins to Talk," introduces the digitally augmented city as a major focus of current design research and practice. In this chapter I critically examine the impact that the entanglement of networked information technologies with the urban realm has produced and discuss this in reference to extant literature. Chapter 3, "Inter*face*, Inter*act*, Improv*act*," is dedicated to models of human-machine interaction that have been influential for the design domain and that form the basis of how we think about designing human-machine interactions today. Chapter 4, "Improvisation as System," examines the nature of improvisation as a concept and practice, drawing on literature from the social sciences, humanities, performance studies, and the emerging field of critical improvisation.

These first four chapters lay the groundwork for chapter 5, "An Improvisation-Based Model for Urban Interaction Design," which articulates four positions for an improvisation-based model of urban interactions in today's hybrid city environments. In chapter 6, "Experimentation with Uncertainty and the Unpredictable," I illustrate this improvisation-based design model through an analysis of a number of recent interactive urban projects that vary in scope and scale. The improvisation-based model offers a different view of these projects that allows for a new understanding of their nature. The richness of practice-based frameworks and improvisation techniques in the performing arts is then explored in chapter 7, "Improvisation as Technique and Practice for Design," where I illustrate how these can become a resource for an improvisation-based design approach by developing a concrete hybrid city application.

The book concludes in chapter 8 with an epilogue, "Toward the Urban Improvise," that reviews the central arguments of the book and reflects critically on living with uncertainty and unpredictability as a form of critical mobility for urban living.

The ongoing smart city discourse often involves a control-oriented perspective based on notions of *planning* and *probability*. Adopting an improvisation-based perspective means, instead, to shift the focus toward *preparation* and *possibility* as well as emphasizing *openness* and *participation*. In this perspective, the role of the designer changes in that it focuses less on technologies as building blocks and more on behaviors and potentialities of both humans and technologies. The book's epilogue is a reflection on the consequences of a performance-based design approach that embraces unpredictability and that is rooted in an idea of working with dynamic *context* and with *situations*. The designer becomes a facilitator of performance, a mediator who does not conclude a work but who instead ensures its ongoing openness.

# 2 WHEN THE CITY BEGINS TO TALK

Whether openly and actively or in subtle, subliminal ways, things talk to us. Tangible and intangible, and at all scales—from the spoon to the city, the government, and the Web, and from buildings to communities, social networks, systems, and artificial worlds—things communicate. . . . Contemporary designers do not just provide function, form, and meaning, but also must draft the scripts that allow people and things to develop and improvise a dialogue.

—PAOLA ANTONELLI, *Talk to Me* exhibition at MoMA

It seems second nature today to consider the built environment of cities as entities that "talk," that can be part of something akin to a conversation, a quick exchange of ideas and information through spoken words, that may even improvise a dialogue in real time. It is a significant departure from a centuries-old consideration of cities as stable entities in terms of their constructed environments, far from the immediacy and quickness of talk. *Aeterna Urbs*, the "eternal city," is how the Roman poet Tibullus (55–19 B.C.) described Rome in his *Elegies*, referring to the city's permanence and persistence.[1] While evolving, cities were not typically associated with the quickness of speech and talk in the way they have come to be seen today.

Before cities were viewed as *talking* entities, they could be *read*. The slower, more reflective act of reading was applied to the city, viewed as an urban fabric made up of streets, squares, buildings, gardens, and waterways—a texture and a text.

For a long time, urbanites read their cities through various forms of maps—abstract representations of their physical structures seen from above. In the mid-eighteenth century, the Italian architect Giambattista Nolli created the *Pianta Grande di Roma,* today commonly known as the Nolli map. It was the most accurate map of the city of Rome when created and was used by the city until as late as the late twentieth century. The map is a figure-ground representation that depicts the city's buildings on the backdrop of the spaces that surround them. The map reveals the relations between public and private spaces in the city. Private buildings are shown in gray, carved into public spaces both covered and uncovered. Interiors of churches read the same way as piazzas and courtyards of palaces. Nolli's map is a representation of the results of the complex processes that are involved in planning and building a city's physical structure. It provides a snapshot in time of this process that knows no end and offers an exclusive focus on the physicality of the constructed environment.[2]

From a different perspective, the urban planner Kevin Lynch's view of the city focused on the mental maps that city dwellers would develop through their direct observation. In his first yet still best-known book, *The Image of the City,* Lynch develops notions of *legibility* and *imaginability,* concepts that would accompany him throughout his career.[3] He identifies five categories that are recurrent in these mental maps: Edges, Paths, Nodes, Landmarks, and Districts. Lynch is interested in how people form their own *image* of a city, an image that is a composite of observed physical space and what we can see and hear: the relation to its surroundings, sequences of events, memory of past experiences, people, and their activities, a composition of fragmentary observations blended with other matters.

Lynch shifts the focus of how the city is read and understood from Nolli's bird's-eye perspective to the sociocultural understanding constructed by a city's inhabitants. He proposes reading "the visual quality of the American city by studying the mental image of that city which is held by its citizens."[4] His focus is on the "legibility of the cityscape," the "ease with which its parts can be recognized and can be organized into a coherent pattern."[5] Lynch suggests that you can read a city like printed text on a page and that both city and text are patterns of symbols that can be visually grasped and understood by their audiences. Reading a city in this way also lays the ground to build cities on the basis of an understanding that inhabitants themselves have of it.

In keeping with the analogy of the city as text, the reading of a text allows for different interpretations every time anew. The text itself, however, remains fixed, especially when printed. This is quite different from the act of writing that generated such a text and even more so from the speech act that may precede the written text.

The philosopher and scholar of everyday life Michel de Certeau looks beyond the city as a text, beyond its legibility. In *The Practice of Everyday Life*, he explores how humans in their everyday practice construct their world by *appropriating* their surroundings in their very own personal and unique ways. De Certeau asserts that larger entities—such as cities—are made up in significant ways by the sum of these individual acts that dissent in regard to the structures set in place by various entities. Inhabitants construct their own and very personal city when they enact connections by walking between places. "The act of walking is to the urban system what the speech act is to language or to the statements uttered."[6] De Certeau focuses on the pluralism of how people actually behave and how they appropriate streets, squares, and buildings in ways that may be different from what planners had in mind. He considers the shortcuts, the ad hoc uses, the improvised acts through which urban dwellers appropriate their city every time anew and in unexpected ways. "The ordinary practitioners of the city live 'down below,' below the thresholds at which visibility begins. They walk—an elementary form of this experience of the city; they are walkers, *Wandersmänner,* whose bodies follow the thicks and thins of an urban 'text' they write without being able to read it."[7] The enunciative function of walking in a city is, for de Certeau, trifold. It involves modes of appropriation by the walker of a topographical system, a form of spatial acting-out of the place, and relations between pragmatic positions or "contracts" embodied by the walkers.

The walkers, for de Certeau, actualize some of the possibilities afforded by the spatial order of a city. They act out where it is possible to walk and where walls or other elements form impediments. The city, for de Certeau, is not the accumulation and arrangement of these physical elements, as those that can be seen and observed in Lynch. Instead, it is what the walkers *make of it* in their act of walking. A city is what its citizens *actually* make of it everyday.

It is that everyday practice, those acts of writing or constructing a city through the unique and personal ways of acting in it, that is today increasingly intertwined with networked information technologies. "The most profound technologies are those that disappear. They weave themselves into the fabric of everyday life until they are indistinguishable from it": this was Mark Weiser's foresight expressed in the early 1990s, and it may have come true at a much larger scale than perhaps anticipated by Weiser himself.[8] As these real-time information networks penetrate even more domains of everyday life, data is generated incidentally to these activities. The city as a built system has reached a new form of *immediacy* in its ability to communicate, to listen, and to express. It does indeed talk, but how and with whom does it talk? What are the topics of such conversations between a city and its inhabitants? Who can raise them, and who can engage?

The sociologist Manuel Castells notes that "the Information Age is ushering in a new urban form, the informational city. Yet, as the industrial city was not a worldwide replica of Manchester, the emerging information city will not copy Silicon Valley, let alone Los Angeles. On the other hand, as in the industrial era, in spite of the extraordinary diversity of cultural and physical contexts there are some fundamental common features in the transcultural development of the information city."[9] Today, the so-called *smart city* concept has come under attack for being technocentric and for pursuing a solutionist approach that is keen on implementing ready-made and technology-based solutions with the promise to solve all kinds of problems while too often ignoring the specificity of the social, historical, institutional, and economic context of a city.[10] The work with networked digital technologies in urban environments needs to become more context specific and resist the one-solution-for-all approach. The turn toward improvisation for the design of urban interactions presented in this book offers such an alternative. It emphasizes context and the specificity of a situation and contrasts the smart city model in that it is characterized by an openness that intrinsically allows for and invites initiative, embracing diversity and otherness in the form of a pluralistic participation of stakeholders.

The entanglement of networked information technologies and urban environments has changed cities and urban life, and it has changed how we think about cities. Over the past two decades, a profusion of terms have been coined by scholars and practitioners to describe aspects of this changing urban condition. *Networked city, real-time city, virtual city, smart city, hybrid city, responsive city,* and *ad hoc city* are terms that are at times used lightly but that have underlying concepts that can help us capture more of the current urban condition and point to ways of working with it.

## NETWORKED CITY

Networks of matter and information pervade today's cities. "The archetypical structure of the network, with its accumulation and habitation sites, links, dynamic flow patterns, interdependencies, and control points, is now repeated at every scale from that of neural networks (neurons, axons, synapses) and digital circuitry (registers, electron pathways, switches) to that of global transportation networks (warehouses, shipping and air routes, ports of entry)."[11] Networks connect people, objects, and places. Electricity is supplied to housing, vehicles, and mobile devices; phone calls are routed to mobile phones; the location of a package is monitored by tags and readers connected to central servers. People, objects, and places are connected unlike ever before.

Cities, however, have always essentially been networks. From the early settlements, people constructed connections between their dwellings and connections between their settlements for the transport of people, goods, and information. The *Viae Romanae,* the public road network of the Roman state, composed of the

Via Aurelia, Via Cassia, Via Tiburtina, and others, connected cities throughout the Roman state's territory. It was a vital network for the development of the Roman Republic and Empire, providing for movement of people and goods as well as for the transmission of information by way of human messengers. Within the Roman city, the *Decumanus Maximus* crosses the perpendicular *Cardo Maximus*, typically at the location of the Forum, the main roads of Roman cities around which the other road network would form to connect the city. The *Viae Romanae* of today are the fiberglass networks that connect the buildings within and between cities. They are the cellphone antennae that blanket significant parts of the globe, enabling communication between people, things, and places.

The networked city is a perspective of today's cities with a focus on the large presence of a multitude of networks, an array of systems that connect diverse sets of entities in diverse modalities. Cable-based high-speed networks provide fast transmission of information. The wireless cellphone network uses a vast array of antennae distributed throughout the territory. Your cellphone negotiates the most efficient tower to connect to, with regard to signal strength and available capacity. Wi-Fi, Bluetooth, and RFID network technologies are other types of wireless networks that devices connect with; each offers different traits with regard to signal strength, reach, transmission speed, and, not least of all, energy consumption. Wireless protocols enable networks to be formed ad hoc. Unlike a desktop computer that is connected via cable, wireless protocols enable devices to connect and disconnect dynamically to networks in automated or user-triggered ways. Different types of these networks are used to offer different functionalities through devices and systems connected to them. Today's network technologies are tightly integrated with the built urban fabric, and ever more of its elements are becoming programmable and uniquely addressable through any one or a combination of networks. The most advanced lighting grids of a city today, for example, address and control each and every street light individually and in distinct ways if required. Connected devices are the nodes of these networks; cables or wireless signals are the links between these nodes. As a proxy, people become connected to these networks via cellphones, electronic tickets, and the like when worn or held. Places become connected to these networks when devices are location aware: when a lamppost in a city square contains information about its specific location and potentially even its orientation or when devices in a room "know" that they are in that room, in that car, on that road, or at that specific latitude and longitude on the global geographic coordinate system.

The connections are not point-to-point but are based largely on the widespread availability of networks of many connections between many points, along which paths are routed and packages of information or matter are being sent. When I order a cup of coffee on my smartphone standing outside a Starbucks café, the order passes from my device via the cellphone network to Starbucks' central server systems, where the information is processed and sent through a landline or cellular telecommunication network to the café that I am about to enter. As the information is brought to the attention of the barista in the café, I will already have entered the café, ready to receive my coffee. In ways such as these, the networked city redefines space and time; it redefines the *here* and the *now*. It also complicates notions of *presence* and *absence*, as I may not have engaged at all with any of the staff throughout this entire process. And it also brings into play notions of privacy, as the information about my presence, my actions, and my choices and preferences are broadcast beyond my immediate awareness and beyond my apparent control.

Embedded sensors can monitor a situation in one place, convey data to another location where data is processed and analyzed, and then connect back to the original location, conditioning the original situation that gave rise to the data being generated in the first place. In the same way, a person acting in a city contributes to dynamics of which others are not aware when making their decisions. Looked on in this way, the networked city resembles what the philosophers Gilles Deleuze and Félix Guattari describe as a *rhizome*. The rhizome is a philosophical network structure in which every part is necessarily connected with every other part of the system. There are no preferential connections because every connection alters the overall network structure. As a consequence, the rhizome cannot be plotted, since the plotting action itself is part of the rhizome, and thus in the very moment of plotting its structure, the structure changes.

Consider, as an example, the scenario from the beginning of the book. A woman is on the way to take the bus. The bus operator monitors the location of buses as well as the number of boarding and alighting passengers in real time. The resulting data points are plotted on real-time maps and used to adjust dispatch and operation of the buses in response to the changing context. Travelers also have access to this information, and therefore, as soon as the system is plotted, the plotting changes the system structure, in that passengers adapt their own mobility tactics. On the basis of the real-time map on the woman's phone, which shows a delayed bus, she chooses to change her plan. She may walk to the stop of another bus line or opt to walk or ride a shared bike for a quicker connection. The sole plotting of the network in the form of real-time maps has become part of this rhizomatic structure, changing the network itself and making any attempt to comprehensively plot the system at any one time impossible.

"The rhizome is an acentered, nonhierarchical, nonsignifying system without a General and without an organizing memory or central automation, defined solely by a circulation of states."[12] What is obtained is a utopian freedom from the constraints of hierarchal systems. The concept of utopian freedom of movement supplied by Deleuze and Guattari has previously been employed by cyber theorists such as Stefan Wray as a means of explaining how users freely move through digital space.[13] While that analysis relates to the internet, it seems that the concept of the nomadic internet user extends quite naturally to explain the city dweller, who, through the use of networked urban technologies, enters, traverses, and leaves real and urban spaces.

An essential part of the Deleuze-Guattari model of the rhizome, however, is that utopian elements can exist only in tension with dystopian forces. The essence of the rhizome is that it exists in contention with arboreal (and, for Deleuze and Guattari, capitalist) interests that seek to curtail the potential freedom presented by the rhizome, and the outcome is a continual battle of territorialism and re-territorialism. This dualism of the rhizome/arboreal model might provide a useful framework for understanding the limits and challenges of current smart city implementations and help ensure that the outcome is the liberated rather than the disenfranchised citizen.

Castells's spatial logic of the *space of flows* is in opposition to *space as place*.[14] It refers to a new economy that, in Castells's terms, is informational, global, and networked. It is a coming together of "the knowledge-information base of the economy, its global reach, its network-based organizational form, and the information technology revolution that has given birth to a new, distinctive economic system." The advanced services that Castells describes and that are enabled by globally networked technologies are "pervasive, and they are located throughout the geography of the planet, excepting the 'black holes' of marginality."[15] Yet, while global, they create different concentrations in different tiers of urban centers, as discussed in Saskia Sassen's seminal study of the joint dominance in global finance and business of New York, Tokyo, and London.[16] The focus is on the urban poles and on the connections between these poles rather than between cities and their territory or hinterlands. "As the global economy expands and incorporates new markets it also organizes the production of advanced services required to manage the new units joining the system, and the conditions of their ever-changing linkages."[17] The networked economy, while being *global* and *networked*, organizes and structures the conditions of the sites in which it manifests itself and that are directly experienced by people. It is not only the connections that the network economy enables but also the different work and leisure practices that it enables at the local level that are significant. It is in this way that the networked economy shapes people's practice and experience in concrete ways.

The *platform economy* is a more recent notion that evolved from conditions described by Castells. Arguably, cities or countries have always been platforms, as a set of principles and a place for encounter of people and things. Today, economists, developers, and designers use the term *platform* to describe the offerings of companies such as Airbnb, TripAdvisor, Uber, and eBay. "A plat-form is a business based on enabling value-creating interactions between external producers and consumers. The platform provides an open, participative infrastructure for these interactions and sets governance conditions for them. The platforms' overarching purpose: to consummate matches among users and facilitate the exchange of goods, services, or social currency, thereby enabling value creation for all participants."[18] In a discussion of platform architecture, Geoffrey Parker, Marshall Van Alstyne, and Sangeet Paul Choudary discuss the importance of openness, which allows for unplanned uses to form meaningful interactions between people mediated by platforms. It is a striking acknowledgment of the value of emergent behavior in the context of interactions using today's digital networks.

One of the key aspects of interactions in a network-based urban context is that information today passes through these networks at high speed, connecting locations, people, and their actions and interactions in real time. Beyond impacting the spa-tial dimension, the hybrid city has indeed changed the way in which we experience *time*.

## REAL-TIME CITY

The term *real time* today is often associated with digital informa-tion technologies. Think, however, for a moment of an encounter with a friend that you meet on the street. You both stop and ex-change a few words: greetings, personal anecdotes, concerns about the weather. In the conversation, you choose your words on the basis of your knowledge of the subject matter, as well as your knowledge of your friend's background. When she frowns, you understand that she disagrees; her gesture informs you that she wants to intervene and respond. You pause to give her an oppor-tunity to speak. You note that your friend is getting impatient when she looks at her watch. She sees that you have noticed her impatience and explains that she has an appointment to get to.

All of this happens in *real time*, through the exchange of many small signals, and does not involve any technology. We are able to capture the dynamics of such interactions effectively, given that the signals exchanged are perceivable and strong enough to be registered and that the encoded information is understood by the recipient.

We engage with environmental information similarly. However, it becomes more difficult with growing distance to the phenomenon of interest or when its signals cannot be registered by the human senses. Consider the road traffic condition at the destination of a route that you are about to start or levels of air pollution along your walk to work. Both are difficult to perceive with human senses alone. Both are also examples of types of information that are available in today's hybrid cities. While systems involved in enabling this kind of information exchange consist of sensors connected to digital information networks and devices such as mobile phones, a key characteristic to enable people to act on such information is the distribution of and access to such information on a *real-time* basis.

What is it, then, that we mean by *real time*? As terms such as *near real time* or *quasi real time* abound, a clarification is worthwhile. Often, the term *real time* refers to a system in which data is processed within a short time interval—for example, a sensor that returns a measurement within a fraction of a second. The difficulty with this approach is that it lacks a specification of the required latency. And this makes it difficult to judge any given system as to whether it does or does not operate in real time.

A more useful definition refers to real time as "the actual time during which a process or event occurs."[19] Consequently, a real-time process implies that there is a deadline before which a given piece of data is useful to the system, whereas that same data is not useful—or may even be destructive—to the system thereafter. While the deadline implies a process, identifying the usefulness of respecting such a process's deadline implies the existence of a higher-level mission. Considering that it is evidently this mission that defines the parameters of the deadline, we end up with an idea of real time in which there is no stringent necessity to speed up data transfer to arbitrarily defined fast levels, but rather the goal is to identify reasonable deadlines for the transmission of information that are related to specific missions. As an example, a three-minute latency of a real-time map showing a city's public transport buses may work sufficiently for an exhibition setting to convey an idea of urban dynamics. The same three-minute latency, however, will be insufficient if the purpose is to inform bus passengers via mobile phones of upcoming bus departure times at stations. With a three-minute delay, the information has passed its deadline of usefulness, and the system has failed to deliver information on time to accomplish the mission, which in this case is catching the bus.

An essential characteristic of a city permeated by networked information technologies that can sense, compute, and act on its environment is that activities can be coordinated in real time, without prior planning, across physical distance and between large numbers of people. And this is a significant change in how we have come to work with time.

Throughout history, humans have developed techniques for keeping time, and the various time-keeping technologies have formed our understanding and our emotional relation to time. "The clock, not the steam engine is the key machine of the industrial age," writes Lewis Mumford.[20] He describes the clock as a machine capable of producing hours and minutes in his historical account of the clock.

Humans have kept track of time for thousands of years, going back to sun and water clocks employed as early as in ancient Egypt. In seventh-century European monasteries, bells rang seven times a day to mark the prayer times. The signaling of what is known as canonical hours brought monks together in their prayers and their collaborative work. Sundials, water clocks, and clocks using falling weights were used to time even and regular intervals between these prayer times. The Benedictine order was on the forefront of regularizing monastic life. Saint Benedict (A.D. 480–550) introduced the *Regula Benedicti* and with it contributed a foundational milestone toward the Western monastic order. Considering that at one point there were forty thousand monasteries under Benedictine rule, the impact that Benedict's monastic order had on its territory, reaching far beyond the walls of the monasteries themselves, cannot be overstated.

The thirteenth century saw the appearance of mechanical clocks throughout Europe, and clock towers in cities were the first to be equipped besides monasteries. They brought mechanical time into the life of merchants and workers in the city. With these mechanical clocks, time-keeping became independent from seasons, daily weather, and light conditions, which challenged earlier time-keeping devices. Mechanical time had become second nature in monasteries, and it contributed to giving human activities the regular collective rhythm generated by the clock. With the widespread use of mechanical time, it became a means to monitor work hours. Work processes can be timed and coordinated through clock time and duration, and they can be planned in advance. Most importantly, however, the clock has become a tool to coordinate and to *synchronize* people's *actions* and *activities* in a way that was impossible before.

As the clock shrinks in size, as in the form of domestic clocks in sixteenth-century England and the Netherlands and in the form of pocket watches in the following century, machine time becomes ever more intertwined with a wide range of everyday activities— so much so that in many ways machine time has come to dissociate time from the temporal dimension of key human events and experiences. Machine time generates an abstract temporal dimension quite distinct from direct human experience. Sun time changes by one minute every mile traveled east or west; a human organism has its own rhythm relating to heartbeat, breath, metabolism. These change in relation to internal and external factors such as levels of health, stress, anxiety, or mood. Today, organic functions have come to be adjusted to machine time, and that in turn has become a new abstract medium of existence. We eat at certain hours rather than when feeling hungry; we go to sleep and wake up in response to time schedules, ignoring somatic feelings of tiredness and wakefulness.

The clock as a machine came to assume a very specific physical configuration. The dial translates the passing of time into movement through space as a clock's hands sweep in a circular motion. Time-keeping became time-accounting and then time-rationing. To reduce the time on any given job, work, or pleasure or to quicken movement through space, this reduction of time consumed by an activity came to be looked on as a sufficient end in and of itself. The clock had indeed become a machine generating seconds, minutes, and hours as products in their own right.

Mumford emphasizes the huge gain in mechanical efficiency enabled through the coordination and articulation of a day's events by the clock, and he stresses that the modern industrial age could do without iron, coal, or steam but not without the clock. Marshall McLuhan builds on Mumford's analysis but recasts the role of the clock for the synchronization of human activity as a reinforcement of literacy—the diffused knowledge of a system of symbols that becomes the basis for synchronization.[21]

The spread of rapid transportation required a further change in the method of time-keeping beginning in the mid-nineteenth century. As sun time varies from place to place, the burgeoning evolution of transcontinental rail transportation led to standard time being adopted in the United States in 1883 following the adoption of Greenwich Mean Time (GMT) by the British railway system across Great Britain in 1847. Never before were human actions, spread over such wide geographic distances, able to move in synchrony. At first, railway time relied on individual chronographs used by station masters and tables that allowed for the conversion between local time and standard time. Soon, however, telegraph lines were installed to synchronize station clocks across the railway system. By 1855, GMT time signals from Greenwich were sent on telegraph lines along railway routes to all stations in Britain. The then-young telegraph technology became an essential ally in conveying time-based coordination across large geographic distances. And it can be seen as an early example of a tight integration between physical infrastructure and information technology that foreshadowed recent developments in today's hybrid cities.

New forms of telecommunication, such as telephone and internet, have since continued this path of supporting ever new forms of coordination among human activity. The connection of machine time with information and communication technologies (ICT) has allowed humans to go beyond boundaries of space and time in synchronizing actions and activities.

As the clock—as a machine for the coordination of human activity—framed people's experience of their world in existential ways,[22] today's hybrid city environments with their real-time technologies frame the way in which we design and think about interactions. Technology-mediated interactions in real time complicate notions of *presence*—being here and elsewhere at the same time. They complicate notions of *awareness*—becoming aware of things that are far away or beyond our sensorial capacity. Real-time interactions enable new forms of response, adaptation, adjustment, and, ultimately, resilience. If information is dynamic and in real time, information can be personalized and hyperlocalized. No two locations or two people receive the same information if that information is time and location specific and in real time, as it will reach distinct locations at distinct moments in time.

In this process, dynamics of *feedback* become key, and the emphasis shifts toward *event time* rather than *metric time*. Actions happen when triggered by relevant events as opposed to abstract time schedules. As an example, streetlights dim and brighten up in reaction to the presence of pedestrians rather than following preset schedules. Event-based interactions mediated by real-time information technologies open up possibilities of working with personal time as part of the coordination of activity across a city.

To revisit space and time in the context of networked communication systems and real-time interactions in urban environments means to shift our way of working with space and time into the sphere of *potentialities*. It essentially means to renegotiate, that is, to *virtualize* them.

## VIRTUAL CITY

The terms *virtual reality, virtual city, virtualization,* and the like often conjure dramatic images of computer-generated illustrations of futuristic cityscapes: computer renderings of skyscrapers in bluish and yellowish color tones, three-dimensional line drawings of underlying CAD models shining through the outer skin of buildings, a simulated sunset to dramatize the fantastic image of a "virtual city." Other times, a "virtual tour" is offered on a screen interface, allowing a user to swipe left and right on an interface and virtually move around an indoor or outdoor space, as in Google's Street View, offering an experience of "being there" without actually being there.

The linguistic origin of the virtual lies in the Latin *virtualis,* derived from *virtus,* and means "force" or "potency." By a scholastic definition, the virtual exists in its potential, not in its act—not actually. The virtual is thus opposite to the actual, not to the real. There is an important distinction between the virtual and the possible.[23] The possible is fully formulated but not yet realized. It will realize without changing anything in its determination and in its nature. The possible is a *fantasmatic real,* in Gilles Deleuze's terms; it is latent. It is exactly as the real but lacks existence. The process of realization is when what happens is exactly what was possible; it is when the possible becomes a reality.

The virtual, instead, is not opposed to the real but to the actual. Unlike the fully formed possible, the virtual is a problematic complex, an intersection of tendencies and forces that accompany a situation, an event, an object, or another entity. It requires a process of transformation, and that process is one of *actualization.* To use one of the media theorist Pierre Lévy's examples, the virtual is like the seed in relation to a tree.[24] The seed is virtually a tree, in that it contains all information necessary for a tree to grow; it contains the whole problem set and all constraints. However, what this tree will *actually* look like depends on many factors and cannot be predicted with certainty. It actualizes as it grows in the context and in the complex interaction with multiple environmental factors. The tree is being invented in a transformative process that is that of an actualization.

In this sense, any actualization is a response to a problem set. It is a solution that was not part of the formulation of the virtual problem complex itself but that has grown out of the process of actualization and its complex interactions within a context. Actualization, then, is *creation*; it is an invention of form that begins with a dynamic configuration of many diverse forces and intentions.

The opposite of the process of actualization is that of virtualization, and this process is of particular relevance to the hybrid city. The pervasiveness of networked information technologies in cities and their activities offers extensive opportunity to work with the process of virtualization as a design approach. Virtualization is the movement opposite to actualization and therefore is the passage from the *actual* to the *virtual*. In line with the linguistic origin of the virtual, virtualization is about increasing a potential. Virtualization is not a derealization; it rather is a change of identity, a change of the way of being, as virtual and actual are but two different forms of being.

Instead of being defined by a solution, an actuality, the process of virtualization leads to an entity that becomes defined by a set of problems. Virtualizing an entity means defining such a general set of problems, starting from an actual form. The original, actual form can be seen as one answer, an actual solution to the problem set that is constructed through the process of virtualization.

An example will help clarify this in practical terms. Let us examine the process of "virtualizing a company," and let us start with what characterizes an actual company in simplistic terms. A company has a building. People go there every day to do their work. These people have offices, and in them there are tables, chairs, and bookshelves to support their work. Sometimes, these workers leave their individual offices and come together in conference rooms for group discussions to coordinate their work. While this is admittedly not the most exhilarating description of a company, it will serve the purpose of this example. A more detailed description of any one specific company and its characteristics will increase the possibilities for an operation of virtualization.

In order to now virtualize this company, we construct each of the foregoing characteristics in terms of a set of problems to be solved. To begin with, a virtual company does not need a building, and it does not need individual offices and conference rooms. Instead, it needs a way for workers to carry out their work individually and to be able to lead conversations with their coworkers at certain moments in their work. The building with its individual offices and conference rooms is only one potential solution to the problem set we just defined. Giving workers laptops and a free pass for coffee at Starbucks for Wi-Fi access and a table might be another form of actualizing what was previously addressed by company-owned offices. A virtual company makes use of a dynamic model of spatiotemporal arrangement in which workers can work from anywhere at any time as long as they can carry out their individual work, coordinate with their coworkers, and so on. Virtualizing a company turns the previously fixed spatiotemporal setup (a fixed building with offices, fixed working hours) into a set of problems to which it continuously invents new solutions, as opposed to having one fixed answer.

The company is one example, but any kind of activity lends itself to be virtualized. Virtualization offers a redefinition of temporal and spatial dimensions of an activity. As we saw in the discussion of the networked city and the real-time city, the use of networked information technologies in cities contributes greatly toward that end. The hybrid city is a formidable context to carry out transformational operations between the actual and the virtual through processes of virtualization and the continuous creation of new forms through actualizations.

The question now becomes how the virtual city is being actualized. Is it an actualization that then becomes a permanent new form of operation, or does such a new form trigger new forms of virtualization in an ongoing cycle?

Actualization is carried out by the *act in the moment*. Deleuze considers the virtual a continuous multiplicity (in that the virtual can at any moment be actualized in many different forms that are qualitatively different) and identifies it with Henri Bergson's notion of *duration*: "[duration] is the virtual insofar as it is actualized, in the course of being actualized, it is inseparable from the movement of its actualization."[25] Actualization is, in this way, an improvised act, in that the outcome cannot be foreseen. Improvisation is a continuum of actualizations of potentialities of a given context. To improvise is to make something out of a situation that was already contained within the situation as a potential—in a similar way as the tree was in the seed, but from the seed alone the actual form of the tree could not be predicted.

The virtual city is the material and immaterial city that is waiting to be actualized in new forms at any time and by the actions of its residents. The virtual city becomes *actualized*, rather than *activated*. It is an actualization in which place, site, and situation are undefined until at any given moment someone can make something out of a place and a moment by acting on it. The open Wi-Fi signal from a café blends over into the nearby public park. That park contains a bench under a tree, and that Wi-Fi signal is available there too. The bench is now a virtual workplace for a passerby who sits down and writes a page of this book over the course of an hour before moving on.

Designing for a virtual city is a shift away from designing for *types* of places.[26] Using architectural types as a guidance to design interactive spaces would mean looking at the formal type of a café to articulate a set of functionalities deemed meaningful in that context. In today's hybrid cities, however, places see usage far beyond the limits of their type, and it is precisely the process of virtualizing activities that contributes to this. Urban information technologies enable activities to happen without any one specific type of place or architecture. Uber enables anyplace along a road to become a taxi stand, Airbnb spreads the notion of hotel over an entire city, and cafés and parks transform into workplaces on demand.

Designing for the hybrid city today means virtualizing the city and the activities it hosts. It does not mean dematerializing it, and it has little to do with fancy computer-generated images of futuristic skylines. It rather means a turn toward the design of *potentialities*.

### SMART CITY

The following scenario, put forth by Mark Weiser in 1991, represents an early proposition of urban-based "ubiquitous computing."

> On the way to work Sal glances in the foreview mirror to check the traffic. She spots a slowdown ahead, and also notices on a side street the telltale green in the foreview of a food shop, and a new one at that. She decides to take the next exit and get a cup of coffee while avoiding the jam.

Once Sal arrives at work, the foreview helps her to quickly find a parking spot. As she walks into the building the machines in her office prepare to log her in, but don't complete the sequence until she actually enters her office. On her way, she stops by the offices of four or five colleagues to exchange greetings and news.[27]

The scenario describes the beginning of a still-ongoing search for new forms, performances, and situations of computing beyond the desktop model—with regard to both the site and the interface metaphor. Weiser's notion of "calm computing," "urban informatics" as proposed by Marcus Foth, "urban computing" as discussed by Adam Greenfield and Mark Shepard, and innovations summarized as the "Internet of Things" are but a few of the new expressions coined to describe the increasing intertwining of digital networked technologies and a diverse range of spaces, contexts, and activities.[28]

When contemplating the domain of digital networked technologies in cities today, the *smart city* concept has gained significant attention across many domains. The term has seen increased use over the past years by scholars and practitioners and points to an ideal of interconnectivity where access to information at any time and in every place enables decisions for the most efficient outcomes.

The concept is in many ways alluring, as it claims to offer solutions to a wide variety of critical urban issues through the implementation of information technologies in the built environment. For once, the technologies considered to tackle these issues appear typically as less costly than previous types of interventions. For example, while previous strategies to alleviate traffic jams would be addressed through the construction of new roads, smart city–labeled approaches would monitor road traffic using data generated by the cellphones that drivers carry in their cars and provide congestion-aware rerouting to alleviate pressure on road capacities. While the cost of new roads in a city is in the millions of dollars for construction and maintenance over the years, software-based transportation solutions claim to ease traffic for a fraction of that cost. Many readers will have witnessed the effectiveness offered by apps such as Waze, Google Maps, and the like to avoid traffic jams while driving. Other readers that live on previously quiet side streets, however, may also have witnessed an increase in traffic due to the algorithm-based rerouting of transit through their neighborhood—an issue that points toward the more complex effects of urban conditions that are often ignored by smart city–labeled initiatives.[29]

The smart city model has evolved into an idea of a city as being akin to a computer.[30] The model represents a perspective on cities in which all kinds of issues can be addressed with software solutions and in which solutions developed once can then be replicated and applied in other cities as well. The alluring elements of this conception are the assumption of bringing the scalability of computer code from the context of a computer to that of a city. As promoted by the Silicon Valley tech start-up culture, the argument goes that it is best to write code once and have it work the same way whether it serves one hundred or a million users. One direct consequence of this perspective has been the idea of developing operating systems for cities as well as the installation of urban control centers.

Technology companies such as Siemens, IBM, and Cisco have supported and driven this model of a smart city, perhaps unsurprisingly, as it opens up an entirely new market for their products and services. Think of the number of computational and networking devices that any of these companies would install once every traffic light, light pole, parking spot, trash receptacle, bench, and so on becomes networked.

A further consequence of this perspective has been the conception of entirely new smart cities built from scratch and by the hands of one single technology supplier or consortium of suppliers, such as in the case of Masdar in Abu Dhabi and Songdo in South Korea. With the use of proprietary technologies and protocols to create an urban information system, the claim is that these cities can respond perfectly to each and every need and desire of the city's residents at any time and in any case.[31]

The belief that citizens' needs and desires can be defined a priori by urban operators instead of being an expression of social interactions that unfold over time is an expression of the top-down control approach for which smart city initiatives get criticized. The position that the sole way to address those needs and desires ought to involve the deployment of networked information systems is another point of critique. More than a critique of the specific technology, it is a critique of a process that eliminates the formulation of a question and a diversity of responses through processes of choice to address any such issue. Smart city interventions are prone to disrupt established processes of democratic decision-making and accountability under the pretense of an algorithmically based drive for efficiency, of which the terms are often not fully known and have not been agreed on democratically. Inhabitants who are subjected to the "smartness" of such urban systems often have little ability to understand the processes and have little agency in the operations, resulting in new forms of disenfranchisement as well as the reinforcement of old forms of disenfranchisement.

The smart city concept presents the very use of technology as an argument for making cities smart, collapsing notions of smartness, competitiveness, and urban entrepreneurialism.[32] The geographers Rob Kitchin and Tracey Lauriault, together with the computer scientist Gavin McArdle, summarize common critiques of the smart city concept in five points: a promotion of technocratic and corporatized forms of governance; the creation of brittle and hackable urban systems; the introduction of forms of panoptic surveillance; the deployment of predictive profiling; and a portrayal of data and algorithms as objective and free from ideology.[33]

A reference that is notably absent from smart city literature is Horst Rittel and Melvin Webber's notion of the *wicked problem*. This is surprising, as all of the issues that smart city initiatives claim to solve are indeed such wicked problems, to which straightforward approaches of problem solving do not apply. For Rittel and Webber, wicked problems are those that are ill defined and that rely on political judgment for resolution. Essentially, they concern all those issues that involve a considerable social component, where different people affected by an issue may have differing views of what the problem actually is and what would be considered a solution. Rittel and Webber view social problems as never to be *solved* as such. Rather, they are *re-solved* over and over again. And that is because wicked problems are highly entangled with every aspect of their specific context. "There is no immediate and no ultimate test of a solution to a wicked problem. . . . Any solution, after being implemented, will generate waves of consequences." Any attempt to solve a wicked problem is therefore necessarily a "one-shot operation." Every attempt at solving the problem conditions its context, which defies methods of learning by trial and error. Rittel and Webber stress that all wicked problems are fundamentally unique and that "every situation is likely to be one-of-a-kind," and they caution that " 'solutions might be applied to seemingly familiar problems which are quite incompatible with them."[34]

Smart city initiatives have been critiqued precisely for a lack of these considerations, for ignoring that they are mostly dealing with wicked problems.[35] The sociotechnical context in which networked digital technologies are deployed determines how well or ill any one implementation will work for a city's residents in practice. While the term *smart city* tends to be used in its singular, it effectively points to an emerging urban condition characterized by an increasingly tight integration of networked digital information technologies within the built urban environment across a broad range of domains, where networks of mobile and embedded devices sense, process, and respond to actions and events that unfold within them. The way that this condition emerges within any one city and in cities around the world varies greatly. This is not surprising, given that cities have always varied greatly, depending on the interplay of a variety of factors, be they geographical, historical, social, economic, cultural, or institutional. The reason that this needs to be critically addressed, however, is that the smart city concept is often for good reason associated with an approach of applying ready-made technology solutions indiscriminately to very diverse urban contexts. Ayona Datta provides one example in her account of the Indian government's goal to build one hundred smart cities. She illustrates how the smart urbanism trope promoted by this initiative is being used to drive aspirations for modernity and development, presenting the smart city as a space for "middling local entrepreneurs who would become the new smart citizens," while evading debate on expulsions of marginalized citizens from their land on a massive scale as cities would be retrofitted with smart transportation, housing, and infrastructure.[36] Nancy Odendaal describes a different dynamic in her critical discussion of the resurgence of a smart city discourse in Cape Town, South Africa, in which municipal governments rather than technology companies appear as the primary agents promoting technology as a social enabler.[37] Beyond the sociotechnical context, these examples highlight the importance of considering the kind of actors that are promoting and coordinating the planning and implementation of networked digital technologies and whose interests these actors represent.

As urban infrastructures and public services increasingly rely on digital networked information systems, the freedom to make use of these networks and the functionalities and services made available by them requires having access to them. William Mitchell describes how what used to be the boundary of the city wall of ancient cities has now become barriers of access to urban information networks.[38] The question is now one of access, about who has what kind of access in the context of the larger discussion on forms of digital divide. The Nobel Prize–winning economist Amartya Sen, in his work on international development, couples issues of access with notions of individual *capability*. Capability for Sen refers to the set of valued "functionings" that a person has effective access to. As a consequence, a person's capabilities represent the effective freedom of an individual to choose between different forms of "functionings" that are valued by him or her and that represent different kinds of life.[39] It is that freedom that C. Z. Nnaemeka addresses in her bold and passionate manifesto when she appeals to designers, developers, and entrepreneurs to turn their attention beyond the much-catered-to "anti-problems" such as the next restaurant or gaming app and instead turn their attention toward what she refers to as the "unexotic underclass" and issues that potentially impact the lives of large parts of society in more significant ways.[40]

Issues of access to information technologies that are at the basis of smart city initiatives also bring into focus a range of issues related to ongoing urban transformations that shift the understanding of urban realities toward more differentiated, polymorphic, variegated, and multiscalar forms. An often overlooked issue in the overall enthusiasm about the increase of the world's population living in cities relates to issues of the more abstract urban/nonurban or the more concrete urban/rural divide, as discussed by Neil Brenner and Christian Schmid as well as by Richard Walker.[41] This perspective points to forms of digital divide that become exacerbated in conditions of the urban that are characterized by an increased integration of digital information technologies in everyday activities and public services. Access to these becomes critical and has important implications in regard to disenfranchised communities and dynamics of exclusion.

## HYBRID CITY

The smart city concept has received ample criticism in regard to the substance of its underlying approach. Beyond this criticism on substance, there is also an issue with its name, which is a good part of the trouble.

The idolization of *smart* began in the 1980s in the context of material science, with the naming of certain materials as smart. *Smart materials* have properties that react to changes in their environment. On the basis of external conditions such as light, pressure, temperature, or electricity, these materials change one of their properties in a reversible way—a prominent example being shape-memory alloys that can be bent and return to an original shape when reaching a certain temperature. The smartness of the behavior of the material was seen in its ability to behave differently in different conditions, responding to context.

Similarly, the term *smart technologies* describes technology systems that are typically composed of sensors, computational devices, and actuators and whose operations and behavior changes based on the sensing of particular environmental conditions. Context, sensing, and adaptation become key concepts, and, again, the smartness of these technologies is seen in their ability to not always operate in the same way but to change some of their behavior in response to contextual conditions.

*Smart materials* and *smart technologies* are two perfectly legitimate terms that project notions of human smartness, as in *being clever and alert,* onto the behavior of materials and technology systems. The issue arises when the same naming scheme is applied to a significantly more complex and multifaceted entity such as a city, which, beyond its material and technological components, involves a social component in its diverse citizenship as well as economic, institutional, and cultural aspects. The attribution of smart to the city causes inevitable confusion and problems, even more so when the claim at stake is that any one technology would grant a city that much-desired label.

The term *smart city,* when used to describe the widespread deployment of mobile and embedded networked information and communication technologies in a city, is problematic essentially because it consists of a value judgment of a specific kind of technology rather than of an outcome. There can simply not be one single name that summarizes all the achievements and failures associated with how any one technology gets used. Instead, there can and probably should be a name that describes the condition of a city pervaded by networked digital information technologies— a condition that is manifest in radically different ways in different cities around the globe but that in many cities shares common traits. It is characterized by a complex intertwining of people, places, things, and information through networked digital technologies. It is a condition that has radically changed the nature of the built environment in today's cities through the integration of a connected fabric of sensors and actuators. It is also a condition of hybridification between the physical city that humans have lived in for centuries and layers of digital data networks that have been added over the past three decades.

"It is becoming increasingly obvious that information is, in important ways, material, and matter is informational," affirms the cultural critic Mark Taylor.[42] Cities have become *hybrid cities,* which tightly integrate digital information technologies within the built environment and which impact many areas of everyday life.

When I suggest to adopt the term *hybrid city*, it is to point to this widespread intertwining of built environment and digital information technologies today. It provides a more neutral term that withholds a value judgment about the role of technology as such. It is a matter-of-fact acknowledgment of the condition of the intertwining of material with the information in our constructed environment. Using the term *hybrid city* allows us to distinguish between the condition of a city pervaded with information technologies, the design models used to work at the intersection of city, people, and technology, and what is actually achieved by such works.

## RESPONSIVE CITY

Over the past decade, the smart city movement has captured municipal administrations, researchers, and technology companies. With an attitude akin to the modernist period in the early part of the previous century and an emphasis on technocentric solutions and the scientific method as a basis to be applied to human endeavors, the focus has been largely on *efficiency*.

A call for a more substantial consideration of human and social aspects in the smart city discourse has more recently moved the focus from *smart city* to *smart citizen*.[43] The shift in focus lies in a de-emphasis of automated action based on predictive algorithms and an emphasis on direct participation of citizens and communities in urban operations supported by information and communication technologies. This shift has put the human component and social dynamics center stage in the work with urban information technologies, responding to the needs, dreams, and aspirations of a city's inhabitants.

In *Smart Cities: Big Data, Civic Hackers, and the Quest for a New Utopia*, inspired by Patrick Geddes's civics, Anthony Townsend advocates for a new civics for the smart city. This new civics comprises thirteen tenets and cautions that "failure to put

people at the center of our schemes for smart cities risks repeating the failed designs of the twentieth century."[44]

Laura Forlano identifies the origin of the simplistic problem-
solution coupling of the smart city concept in an underlying
human-centered design approach. While a human-centered approach in design was seen as overcoming a focus on making the
technology work for its own sake, human-centered design all too
quickly settled on satisfying problems for individual users of
devices or services while ignoring more complex and significant
underlying sociotechnical intricacies. Forlano advocates for an
integration of participatory design and speculative design approaches with the human-centered design approach and suggests
"decentering the human and nonanthropocentric design to think
through ways designers can evolve existing human-centered design
(HCD) methodologies to contend with socio-technical complexity—such as economic and ecological crisis—and create more
responsible, accountable, and ethical ways of engaging with
emerging technologies."[45]

The umbrella term *responsive city* refers to a number of initiatives and positions that argue for information technologies to
facilitate a more responsive interaction between citizens and the
multiple public and private stakeholders involved in shaping urban
life. *Responsiveness* in this context refers to both how actors
that drive urban operations engage with citizens and also how
networked digital technologies can be employed in a more context-
aware way, acting in response to specific conditions of their environment. The responsive city in this sense proposes to create a
link between urban technology innovations and lessons learned
in regard to citizen and community participation. The objective
is to create cities that are competitive and agile as well as resilient
on several levels but especially on a social dimension.[46]

While citizen participation is a key component of initiatives
under the responsive city umbrella, the way participation is
considered in this context varies considerably.[47] Frequently, participation is seen as little more than compliance to expected behaviors identified as desirable by others. Strategies of nudging or

incentive-based systems are examples of this. They typically use monetary rewards or different types of social currency.[48] The essence of these forms of participation is that they are based on the identification of desired behavioral forms. On the basis of those aspirational forms of behavior, strategies are developed to incentivize citizens to comply to these forms and see value in such compliance for themselves. This is often done with the best intentions, if you consider incentives to change daily routines to lower household energy footprints or commuting emissions. Nevertheless, the modality of participation from the side of citizens is limited to the adherence to standards formulated without their direct involvement.

Another form of participation is the involvement of citizens as a source of information.[49] Through the use of different kinds of information systems (web based, smartphone apps, etc.), feedback is solicited with the objective of capturing people's evaluations of certain events, circumstances, and conditions. Retrieving citizen feedback in digital formats allows also for an efficient integration with other data-driven systems.

Yet another form of citizen participation is the direct involvement of citizens in the planning and management processes of urban services. Municipalities and urban operators have an interest in seeking active citizen involvement of this kind, as they benefit from their location-specific knowledge. On the basis of citizens' deeper understanding of local context, administrations and urban operators are able to plan for and provide interventions, infrastructures, and services that have a higher chance of meeting actual needs, requirements, and aspirations of those who will be impacted. Also, as people are more involved directly in processes of planning service provision, they tend to have a higher sense of ownership of and satisfaction with these services.[50]

The shift toward a responsive city means putting the needs and dreams of citizens front and center. The smart city concept has revived modernist notions of technology as a solution per se, regardless of context and with the ability to automatically foster economic prosperity, as well as equal and efficient governance.[51] A responsive city, instead, builds on the participation of citizens in addressing issues of importance to their context. Even more, it turns to citizens to understand what issues are of importance. Citizens in various professional and informal roles can then develop meaningful and innovative approaches to address these issues with the support of technologies rather than considering the use of technology as innovative in itself.

The use of responsive technologies in cities does not, then, end with the implementation of the technologies but can be seen as a continuum, as information is being exchanged via these systems between sensors in urban environments and the various connected stakeholders. The way that these information exchanges evolve over time becomes as much a part of such a project as the implementation of its initial system setup. Stakeholders change, as do the issues to be addressed. Technology in the responsive city needs to evolve along with changes in the city that it is itself a part of. The terms and goals of the technology deployment will change over time. In such a context, a goal-driven efficiency approach, as suggested by the smart city concept, becomes difficult to sustain and justify.

Eric Gordon and Stephen Walter, scholars of digital civic engagement, challenge the value attributed to efficiency in today's hybrid cities with their seemingly paradoxical concept of *meaningful inefficiencies*. They shift the focus toward inefficiencies as a mode of operation that opens up a space for "letting unexpected issues emerge and take center stage" and that creates distance from a goal-driven efficiency paradigm. The concept of meaningful inefficiencies can be applied to "any process wherein efficiency is deprioritized in favor of relation, connection, or reflective practice."[52]

The approach is inspired by the domain of games, where systems of rules often compel the user to choose the least efficient over the most efficient means of achieving goals. Games are, by definition, inefficient systems, notes Gordon. He gives an example from Bernard Herbert Suits's book *The Grasshopper* about golf as an activity geared toward choosing the most inefficient way of reaching the game's goal: we could just carry the ball to the hole but instead choose to hit it with a club, putting trees, lakes, and other obstacles in between. These rules do not make the game more efficient; rather, inefficiencies make the game more *meaning-ful*. Game systems are defined by inefficiencies to create the meaning of the game.[53] "Meaningful inefficiencies" create space for meaning-making in the pursuit of an undertaking. This is different from "mere inefficiencies," which do not involve processes of meaning-making but rather result in a process taking longer, without any gain in meaning.

Deciding to give space to inefficiency means embracing dynamics and interactions that are different from a norm, that are a deviation. It creates a space for interactions that are essentially unique and established on an ad hoc basis, born from within a specific context and meaningful to those who are involved.

## AD HOC CITY

When things connect in the hybrid city, they do so mostly intermittently. People, things, and places are not permanently connected in the hybrid city. They connect when a situation or an opportunity arises; they happen in an ad hoc way. When required, the connection is quickly established between mobile or embedded digital devices. Information is exchanged, computations are executed, new data are analyzed and compared to existing data sets, and as a response to all of this, actions are triggered.

Take, for instance, the use of electronic tickets for public transportation. While you may be carrying your e-ticket inside your pocket all day long, the only time that ticket connects to anything is when you bring it close to the turnstiles at the subway entrance. The radio-frequency-based system at the turnstile sends out a signal to your card, and your card reflects that signal with its code as part of this response. On the basis of the information received from your card, the transport operator's ticketing system verifies payment and opens the turnstile or sees insufficient payment and blocks entry. Beyond that local interaction, the electronic ticketing system may also operate a passenger count, which then may impact train frequency as a short-term decision as well as any kind of longer-term planning intervention based on overall aggregate passenger numbers.

Another example is the bike-sharing systems that have seen rapid deployment in many cities in recent years. Several attempts in the 1990s and early 2000s in some European cities failed,[54] but bike-sharing systems are currently seeing an aggressive revival. Two main types of these systems have emerged, one using bike docks, the other as a dockless format. The dock-based format is particularly interesting for a view of the city as an ad hoc city, in that its functioning is based on ad hoc interactions both at the level of digital wireless systems and in the material context of the city. Dock-based bike-sharing systems typically use bike docks that are not permanently anchored to the pavement. Instead, they are moveable and relocatable and are in fact often relocated in an ad hoc way by the operator in order to tune the dock locations on the basis of usage patterns. On the user front, these bike-sharing systems represent a formidable ad hoc possibility to ride a bike without owning one and without going through a lengthy rental process in any one fixed location. Instead, as an urban dweller, you tend to stumble upon these docks. With the electronic card of the system or by using one's banking card, the transaction is completed in a matter of seconds, and one is able to ride off with a bike that can then be left at any other dock station in the city, the locations of which are found on a map-based smartphone app.

Ad hoc is typically seen as the foe of efficient operation. It signifies an operation that is not applicable to anything else but the one specific instance. Literally, *ad hoc* means "for this," and it describes something that is formed or carried out for a particular purpose only. It is not meant to apply in the same way to other purposes and defies typical notions of efficiency because it is not generalizable. However, that point of view is being challenged at the moment, in that technology-mediated interactions at an urban scale are impacted by dynamics of customization and demand-responsiveness. Numerically controlled manufacturing processes are today able to manufacture individualized products at scale and, similarly, demand-responsive services can cater at scale to the unique circumstances that arise for any one individual customer.

An urban example of such a shift toward customization and ad hoc operation is the system of demand-based waste collection from public waste bins, such as those developed by the Massachusetts-based company Big Belly. Instead of having a city's waste-collecting trucks go on a fixed route to empty public waste bins a set number of times per day, the company's waste bins are equipped with sensors and powered by photovoltaics. Via a cellular network connection, the waste bins communicate with a central server, sharing data about how full they are in real time. On the basis of actual usage, a city's waste-collection trucks are then sent out only when needed, on an ad hoc basis. What at first seems a small change involves a radical shift of perspective for urban administrations on service provision, from a quantitative (collect waste a fixed number of times per day) to a qualitative perspective (collect waste as often as is required to maintain an agreed-on level of cleanliness).

Charles Jencks and Nathan Silver have brought notions of ad hoc into the context of architectural discourse in their 1972 book *Adhocism: The Case for Improvisation*, which was recently reissued.[55] Adhocism in the 1960s was a reaction to the monotony of the emerging mass market, to the production of mass-produced artifacts and cultural products aimed at as large an audience as possible, which was seen as an attempt to produce the same for everyone. "Our hope was that, in place of market stereotyping, a more creative pluralism would emerge. We wanted to persuade consumers to create their own hybrids, to enjoy the bricolage made possible by the proliferating choice of world production, to personalize what was becoming an anodyne globalism—globcult."[56]

Adhocism, instead of focusing on moments of consumption, privileges moments when actual creation occurs. Adhocism celebrates when two or more elements are brought together in a new constellation, unprecedented and with a surprising outcome. Arthur Koestler likened the act of creation to a good joke: the formulation of a connection between two reference frames that are not usually linked and that generate a new, unexpected impact as a result.[57] The result is a surprising comic effect in the case of a joke and an innovation in the case of a creative idea.

The hybrid city, with its potential for connections between people, things, and places, appears to offer a renaissance for notions of adhocism in cities today. Is Archigram's Plug-In City becoming alive in the hybrid cities of today? The British avant-garde architecture collective in the 1960s proposed a series of provocative hypothetical projects that explored the potential of then-unrealized technologies to allow for new forms of flexibility within enormous structural frameworks. Instead of the physical megastructure proposed then, the plug-in city of today relies on contactless plug-ins with wireless protocols and physical-digital hybrids. A café becomes a workspace because of available table space and a Wi-Fi connection; bike-sharing docks are relocated to cater to changing use patterns, while the cellphone-based technology of the dock keeps track of its own location while facilitating information exchanges between dock, bikes, users, and operator; digital avatars in virtual mobile game environments such as Pokémon Go generate meeting spots for actual gatherings of players without any physical signage or structure.

In the ad hoc city of today, food trucks are locatable on a phone's map, turning open public spaces into temporary restaurant venues. Inflatable bubbles such as *Spacebuster* by Berlin-based Raumlabor or *The Truth Booth* by Cause Collective turn unoccupied spaces into gathering venues for citizens to discuss pressing issues while digitally networking those conversations beyond the local.

City-making has moved beyond the practice of urban planners to include citizens starting to think and act in new ways, inspired by strategies of bottom-up governance. Urban planners have adapted new vocabularies including strategies and tactics of pop-up urbanism, boosterism, and notions of place-making.[58]

When people, things, and places can be and are connected throughout the urban fabric, small local interventions can have significantly larger impacts beyond their apparent scale. The art and design studio Rebar put up its first on-street parking installation in San Francisco in 2005. What followed was the now annually occurring event of Park(ing) Day in cities around the globe, reclaiming hundreds of parking spots in cities for impromptu activities. Park(ing) Day paved the way in San Francisco for the Parklets initiative. Businesses and associations formally claim on-street parking for installations outside their storefront that are for use by their clients but also always open to the general public.

The hybrid city has become a condition of the urban that is already characterized by a context that enables and invites people to improvise with and within the urban environment. Once people, places, and things can connect in multiple ways, the participation by citizens in reconfiguring these connections brings about unexpected outcomes that are to a high degree context and situation specific. Improvisation—as a technologically enabled practice and as a concept—is becoming central to the design of interactions in today's hybrid cities. To understand how improvisation works is becoming essential to understanding emergent practices of human interactions in cities and to design systems and artifacts that can play their role in this new urban condition. The improvisation-based model for design in hybrid city environments presented in the following chapters of this book offers precisely such a perspective, by emphasizing context, agency, and the specificity of a situation. The improvisation-based model is contrasted with the smart city model, in that it is characterized by an *openness* that intrinsically allows for and invites *initiative* by participants and that embraces *diversity* and *otherness* in the forms of participation by a pluralism of stakeholders.

# 3  INTER*FACE,* INTER*ACT,* IMPROV*ACT*

It's not that the audience joins the actors on the stage; it's that they become actors—the notion of observers goes away.

—BRENDA LAUREL, *Computers as Theatre*

Digital networked technologies have become increasingly pervasive in today's urban environments. But regardless of the urban dimension, the domains of human-computer interaction (HCI) and interaction design have long examined design approaches that take into account the ways in which humans relate to technologies. Different ways of thinking about the interaction between humans and machines have informed the way we work with technologies. The mental models we adopt when working with technologies contribute not only to how we view them but also to how we shape these technologies in substantial ways.

As an example, developers in the early phase of the industrial age had a keen interest and preoccupation with manufacturing processes made possible by newly developed power-driven machines. This focus on manufacturing led to an emphasis on *how to manufacture* artifacts with these new machines, which became a dominant driver for the form of objects themselves. Differently today, user-centered design approaches have become more widely embraced, putting a focus on *usability* up front in the development of new products. This does not mean that issues related to production processes are ignored today—far from it. Rather, the emphasis and perspective in the design process have shifted. The contrast is evident when considering the harsh working environments of train drivers and stokers in nineteenth-century steam trains compared with the more humane working environments in cockpits of the most recent high-speed trains in Europe and Asia. One was constructed in the context of a manufacturing-centric view, while the other stems from a human-usability-centric view.

Looking at this example more closely, we can identify further distinctions in how to contemplate human-machine interactions. We can identify the interaction of the driver and stoker in terms of an *immediate* and *embodied* form of *action*. These consist in the stoker's handling of a shovel, a direct vision of the fire in the furnace and the process of supplying coal in response to the direct observation of fire and train movements. Today's train drivers, instead, interact with their machine in a *mediated* way that is afforded by interfaces such as dials and digital screens, using symbolic and representational models. In regard to the design of these interfaces, we can adopt an interface-centric view that focuses on the information design of dials and screens as something that stands in between the machine and the human user. Alternatively, we can adopt *performative* notions of action and interaction if we expand the view on the human-machine interaction of driver and train beyond dials and screens and consider a driver's daily routine, behavior, and experience more comprehensively. The point is that whichever view we adopt will significantly impact the outcome of working on the interaction between humans and technology, and this remains the case also for networked technologies in today's urban environments.

## A SURFACE IN BETWEEN

When considering the interaction with digital technologies today, flat screens and their graphical components immediately come to mind. The graphical user interface (GUI) continues to be the predominant mode of interacting with computers, whether they be desktop-based systems or mobile devices. Developed beginning in the 1960s and 1970s, GUIs were introduced in mainstream products after initial development done at Xerox Palo Alto Research Center (PARC) and for Apple's Macintosh computers in the 1980s.

Users interact with electronic devices through GUIs by manipulating graphical elements such as windows and menus. When developed, GUIs were a step to overcome the significant learning curve that previous command-line interfaces such as the operating systems Unix and MS-DOS required from users. GUIs leverage the familiarity that people have with everyday environments and employ metaphors from such environments—desktop, windows, and others—to facilitate interface-mediated human-machine interactions.[1]

The interface as a conceptual model for interacting with machines, however, is broader than just the GUIs found on screens of electronic devices. Car dashboards are a prominent example of an interface. Dials translate speed and revolutions per minute (rpm) values into the position of hands on marked dials that facilitate a numeric readout. The clock is another familiar example. A complex set of interlocking gears and springs ensures constant rotation, but we do not *read* time from those gears but from its interface made up of a dial and hands. Clocks make time spatial and quantifiable because of the specific interface through which it is presented to us.[2] The passage of time is translated into the circular motion of hands that divide a circle into minutes, quarters, and halves. An interface represents the workings of the machine through the use of a system of symbols—"it was not the clock, but literacy [of a symbolic system] reinforced by the clock, that created abstract time and led men to eat, not when they were hungry, but when it was time to eat."[3]

Consider for a moment the door handle you used when entering the room you sit in right now—that is an interface also. The tap on your water faucet that you turn and lift to adjust temperature and flow strength is also an interface. Interfaces are effective ways of representing the workings of machines when such workings are not easily understood without a translation of its functioning or when direct sensory perception (sight, hearing, smell, taste, touch) is obstructed or restricted.

The interface is a particularly effective conceptual model when configurations of human-product interactions remain constant, as is the case for physical sliders, levers, dials, handles, and the

like. Testimony to this is the use of graphical interface elements
in the shape of buttons, levers, sliders, dials, and handles, which
leverage the familiarity with their physical equivalents and which
are employed even in the interfaces of most sophisticated computational devices.

More broadly still, interface as a conceptual model describes
an entity, a *face*, that is located *in between* (*inter-*) two or more
systems at the point of their encounter. The interface is a *surface*
that presents a view of one system to another system. It *represents*
one system to the other, be it a machine or a human. To design
an interface requires an understanding of both systems, of how
they operate and function, and of how each interprets and makes
sense of the other system.

Focusing on the interface means focusing on *where* two systems face each other. The interface is effective in *locating* a zone
of interaction between two systems, between human and machine.
This focus, however, also de-emphasizes other aspects that exist
beyond that moment and that place of facing each other. In
fact, the term *user* is a consequence of this confined focus on a
zone of interaction. It is geared toward a utilitarian and task-
orientated approach to conceiving human-machine interactions.
Interface is a zone that is controlled and controllable, where certain actions can be performed and others not. Interface is therefore
a model that implicitly considers a highly controlled and con-
strained area of action.

Beyond the cognitive interaction, the interface prescribes a
certain way of posing one's body toward the machine. An interface
requires that it be *faced*. One needs to face an interface in order
to interact through it with the machine. Further, the interface sets
the terms for such an interaction, what can be done and what not
and also how and when specific tasks can be performed.

This focus on a specific location and orientation is a challenge
when working with the interface model in the context of urban
interactions. The location of interaction with a technology system
in urban environments is typically *spread out* and *fragmented*.
Think, as an example, of transportation systems. To work with
kiosk-based interfaces, digital signage boards, and the like is

ultimately a cumbersome and stifling approach when dealing with an activity such as transportation or travel that involves change at various levels: movement of people and vehicles, movements that occur at different moments and in different places, and movement that happens at diverse speeds. At different instances and in different situations, people will interact in very different ways with elements of transportation systems, and these interactions will unfold very different meanings over time and as people move through the city.

As people work and interact with technologies, they change, they evolve, and they learn. Dealing with technologies changes the human user as well as the technology with regard to the role those technologies play in an actual context. The interface as a conceptual model involving an entity that stands *in between* the human and the machine is challenged when the interaction is more spread out. This is where other models come into play that consider *actions* and *activities* in a more comprehensive way.

## CONVERSATIONS AND COMMON GROUND

While interface is an effective conceptual model to contemplate various human-product interactions, especially when configurations are fixed, the plasticity of the nature of human-computer interfaces has led to the development of alternative models for conceptualizing interaction.

The notion of conversation as a model for interaction describes situations in which meaning is *negotiated* and *co-created* through processes of interaction between humans and between humans and computers. Here, humans and computers do not simply represent themselves to one another. Instead, a conversational model considers a shared context for action in which both are agents in an Aristotelian sense. Both are capable of taking action, and meaning arises from the interaction of the agents in context in an ongoing way.

Common ground theory is based on work developed by Herbert Clark in the field of communication theory.[4] It describes how successful collective human action consists in an ongoing coordination of content and process based on "mutual knowledge, mutual beliefs, and mutual assumptions" that constitute the common ground among participants. Common ground is not predetermined and static but dynamic, and it accumulates over time: "All collective actions are built on common ground and its accumulation."[5]

In linguistics and psychology, common ground is considered a shared knowledge and understanding that underpins the successful communication between people, involving the spoken word as well as posture, gestures, and expressions. It is assumed and tested in an ongoing form throughout a conversation, a form of collaborative action. Affirmations are made and reactions (both verbal and nonverbal) are observed to confirm elements of shared understanding and those that require further explanation. Successful further explanation will then contribute to increase the common ground between participants. Coordination occurs in the process (waiting for the right moment to speak up, to listen, to nod, etc.) as well as in the content (making a new reference and attending to the reaction, changing the reference, explaining a reference, etc.): "Accomplishing this, once again, requires the [participants] to keep track of their common ground and its moment-by-moment changes."[6]

*Grounding* is the process by which participants in a conversation update their common ground as the interaction unfolds. This takes the form of asking a question, affirming that the question was understood, obtaining a response to that question, and confirming that the answer is mutually understood. Two main factors that shape grounding as discussed by Clark and Brennan are *purpose* (what the participants want to accomplish) and *medium* (the means of communication through which the conversation occurs).

Common ground theory has been used for human-computer interaction to give room to the nuances and subtleties of human interaction.[7] It has also been used to address issues of establishing intersubjective understandings in the design of interactive technologies with regard to "communication between a designer and a user" and communication "*between* users, *through* the system."[8]

The use of conversation as a model for human-machine interaction can be traced back further to the work of Gordon Pask on *conversation theory* beginning in the 1970s.[9] Pask's theory is based on his work with cybernetics and represents a constructivist epistemology that looks at how we learn and how knowledge and understanding are constructed. Meaning is agreed on by way of conversation, and responses depend on one entity's interpretation of the behavior of another entity. Pask identifies precedents to his theory in the work of the psychologists Jean Piaget and Lev Vygotsky.[10] Human-machine interaction modeled after human conversation becomes a dynamic process in which human and nonhuman participants learn about each other. A fundamental idea of Pask's theory is that learning itself occurs through conversation and that conversation serves to *make knowledge explicit*.

Both common ground theory and conversation theory suggest models in which meaning is negotiated and co-created between humans and computers through interactions. Unlike Clark's work on common ground, for Pask, the construction of a shared understanding or grounding does not require either *purpose* or *medium* a priori. Instead, Pask identifies *intention* as key in conversation, acknowledging that the goal or purpose itself can be underspecified. In fact, the purpose of a conversation may become apparent only through the conversation.

Pask himself applied conversation theory in his work on computational machines, such as *The Colloquy of Mobiles* developed for the 1968 exhibition *Cybernetic Serendipity* at the Institute of Contemporary Arts in London. A responsive, computer-based system was suspended from the ceiling, and the five mobiles communicated with each other by way of flashlights and mirrors. This formed a kind of social system, an environment with an *aesthetic potential*. Pask collaborated extensively with architects throughout his career. He was invited to join the team for the Fun Palace project by the architect Cedric Price and the theater director Joan Littlewood. At MIT, Pask was a member of the nascent Architecture Machine Group, founded by Nicholas Negroponte in 1967, which went on to become the MIT Media Lab, an interdisciplinary research laboratory devoted to the convergence of technology, art, and design. More recently, Ranulph Glanville, Paul Pangaro, Usman Haque, and Hugh Dubberly, among others, have carried forward Pask's work in the context of architecture and interaction design. Conversation as a design model for human-machine interaction has gained significant attention lately in the context of speech recognition and conversational interfaces in the form of Apple's Siri, Amazon's Alexa, and their other talkative machine-based colleagues.

Pask invests the architect or designer with the role of designing systems, instead of buildings that follow rigid typologies. As the occupants of the built environment change, evolve, and adapt, Pask sees an imperative for these structures to reach similar capabilities to remain relevant and effective. In his *cybernetic design paradigm*, he articulates the following design stages for the construction of *adaptive environments*: (1) specification of the purpose or goal of the system (with respect to the human inhabitants), where the goal may be underspecified with the aim to provide a set of constraints that allow for certain modes of evolution; (2) choice of the basic environmental materials; (3) selection of the invariants that are to be programmed into the system with regard to what properties will be relevant in the human-environment dialogue; (4) specification of what the environment will learn about and how it will adapt; (5) choice of a plan for adaptation and development or a number of evolutionary principles.[11]

It falls to the designer of such a system to specify what the environment will learn about, how it will learn, and how the focus of its learning will be able to evolve over time on the basis of evolutionary principles. The designer of adaptive environments, as discussed in Pask's writing, will thus not be designing the environment as such but rather the terms on which such an environment organizes itself over time and in an ongoing interaction with its human occupants and other factors. The designer, in this view, loses his or her position as a controller and, instead, instills his or her creations with the structural and procedural capabilities to respond and to evolve.

## ACTIVITY IN CONTEXT

Developments in the social sciences in the 1980s challenged the interface as a model for human-machine interaction. They brought about a shift in focus away from interface and toward *interaction* and larger notions of *activity* that machines are part of. They focused on *context* within which such interactions happen. In this perspective, it is not enough to consider the graphic elements that represent a machine's functionalities to a user posed in front of the machine. The machine is considered part of dynamic and complex sociocultural processes. It takes on a role within this context and becomes an agent, an actor.

Similar to *inter*face, *inter*action points to an action in between and describes what goes on between humans or humans and artifacts. As part of this interaction, both human and artifact act on each other in a subject-object constellation. They are related to each other as part of an activity that involves them both. "Interaction (that is, face-to-face interaction) may be roughly defined as the reciprocal influence of individuals upon one another's actions when in one another's immediate physical presence."[12]

An important stage in this turn toward interaction and context is represented by the work of Lucy Suchman, the former founding member and manager of the Work Practice and Technology area at Xerox PARC. Suchman's work there involved ethnographic studies of everyday practices involved in the design and the use of technology.[13] The predominant cognitivist approach to human-computer interaction and artificial intelligence at the time Suchman wrote her seminal book *Plans and Situated Actions* was a plan-based model.[14] The idea, which Suchman contrasted in her work, was that humans essentially think up a plan of what to do and then execute this plan in a step-by-step approach, evaluating feedback to correct the action to remain on task. An example for this model of action is Donald Norman's *Seven Stages of Action*. Norman's seven stages are goal, plan, specify, perform, perceive, interpret, and compare. The first four are associated with execution and the latter three with evaluation. Norman was explicit that this model is "simplified, but it provides a useful framework for understanding human action and for guiding design."[15] The seven stages for Norman were the plan, the script for a sequence of actions through which humans engaged with their world. The plan-based model lent itself very well to the programming of machines. The idea was that any human action could be broken down into a sequence of action steps, and more complex actions may be broken down into further substeps.

What Suchman did in her work was to radically question the assumed stability and objectivity of the phenomena in the world and the interactions of humans with them as a key assumption of the planning model. She substituted this assumed stability and permanence with a human engagement with the world that involves an active and continuous interpretation of that world. This active engagement is highly dependent on its specific context and setting. Situation and context take center stage: "the sequential organization of behavior, in Suchman's model, is an ongoing, improvised activity."[16]

Suchman draws on ethnographic research into the practices of Micronesian seafarers navigating the open waters surrounding the Caroline Islands in critically assessing the role of plans in shaping directed courses of action. She contrasts the fixed and universal plan of the European navigator to courses of action taken by the Trukese that are "contingent on unique circumstances that he cannot anticipate in advance."[17] The course is guided by moment-to-moment interaction with the immediate context; actions are temporally contingent and situationally aware. The plan, then, is manifest only after the fact and becomes an ex post account of the course taken.

Suchman argues that "purposeful actions are inevitably *situated actions*," actions taken in the context of concrete and specific circumstances.[18] "We must act like the Trukese because the circumstances of our actions are never fully anticipated and are continuously changing around us."[19] Plans, in this perspective, become a resource for action rather than a prescriptive frame for action itself. They play a role before the action, as a tool to put oneself in a good starting position, and they play a role after the action, as a means to narrate and account for the action that has taken place. They do not, however, determine the course of actions.

The concept of situated action ties human action to its context but essentially leaves the subject-object constellation intact. An interaction arises on the basis of a consideration of a human subject capable of action and an artifact object, which are linked by a specific activity. The work summarized under the term *activity theory* complicates this relation.[20] It shifts the constellation from one in which subject and object are a pre-given to a subsequent interaction and activity toward a view in which subject, object, and activity are mutually dependent in an existential triad. It is interaction between subject and object as part of an activity that forms both subject and object. The focus is now on *activity*, which, for activity theory, becomes the basic unit of investigation in order to understand both subject and object.

To understand how an activity forms both subject (the human) and object (the technological artifact), Victor Kaptelinin and Boni A. Nardi give the example of a weight lifter.[21] Will a weight lifter be sufficiently strong to lift a certain weight? Might he or she be too weak or the weight too heavy? Activity theory approaches an activity as a *transformative* event. Weight lifters regularly lift weights that are beyond their capacity as part of their training. By doing so, they deliberately provide their organism with a shock that promotes muscle growth. This activity of lifting too heavy weights thus shapes the subject. It transforms the weight lifter, and when lifting a weight again the next time, the weight lifer will have changed: his or her muscles will have grown. The activity will have transformed the subject. The object will also have changed in relation to the subject; the weight will appear to have become lighter. There will not be any identical instance of such an activity. At any subsequent encounter between that weight lifter and that weight, their relation will have changed by the first activity of lifting that weight.

Activity theory traces its roots to the work of Piaget and Vygotsky—notably the same scholars Gordon Pask identified as an early reference to his work on conversation theory. Human activity is contemplated as a systemic and socially situated phenomenon.

Focusing comprehensively on an activity overcomes both a narrow focus on technology alone and a limiting setup between one individual user and a device.

Kaptelinin and Nardi in their conclusion point to a future direction in research that considers "environments as mediators of human interaction in the world," suggesting that "as designers, we construct environments to help people get something done; we think of them as mediators of activity. Making the relationship between artifacts, environments, and the world an object of analysis and extending the notion of mediation beyond tools are promising and much-needed directions for the further development of activity theory."[22]

This reflection presents a direct link to the work summarized as *mediation theory*. Its roots are based in the young domain of postphenomenology, whose central focus is the kinds of relations that humans can have with technologies.[23] The domain draws on phenomenology and pragmatism, analyzing the role of technologies in social, personal, and cultural life by way of studies of concrete technology examples. It is based on phenomenology's focus on experience, the recognition of the role of *embodiment*, and the situation of experience in a lifeworld of specific epochs and locations. From pragmatism, the field embraces the view of consciousness as an abstraction, of experience as an organism-environment model that is embedded in the material world and a cultural-social dimension. As a third component, postphenomenology embraces the empirical turn put forth by developments within the philosophy of technology centered on Hans Achterhuis's work.[24] The distinctions from a more traditional philosophy of technology consist in a move from a concern for technology in general terms toward the specific and the peculiar in the analysis of technology case studies. Postphenomenology moves from a nostalgic rejection of technological changes toward considering technology as an integral part of the cultural constellation. Postphenomenology adopts a constructivist view of technology that goes beyond taking technologies as a given. It instead analyzes concrete processes of development and formation that involve diverse actors and social forces acting on the creation of technology, which results in a view of the co-evolution of technology and society.

In the analysis, then, of the kinds of relations that humans can have with different technologies and how reality's presence to humans is shaped by technologies, the two dimensions discussed by Peter-Paul Verbeek, following Don Ihde's work, are hermeneutical and existential.[25] In hermeneutical terms, artifacts mediate the way in which humans have access to the world in ways that require interpretation. This dimension is concerned with questions such as the way in which others are present to us when we communicate to them through information technologies or how we have access to the world through tools such as maps, the microscope, a night-vision system, and so on. In existential terms, human existence is mediated by artifacts, and the focus is on questions such as how information technologies impact our social relations and how technologies such as the cellphone condition how we perceive and work with time and as a consequence structure our day.

Ihde starts his analysis of the relation between human beings and their world with experience. He distinguishes two dimensions of experience that are always co-present, that cannot be separated, and that mutually require each other: (1) micro-perception, or the bodily experience on a sensory level; and (2) macro-perception, or the framework within which the sensory perception becomes meaningful. Using these two dimensions of experience, the postphenomenological perspective articulates different kinds of relations between humans and their world, afforded by technologies, while putting particular emphasis on the mediating character of tools and technologies. Ihde proposes a taxonomy of four different kinds of such relations that can exist between humans and their world when artifacts are involved; this list was extended by Verbeek to a total of seven kinds: embodiment relation, hermeneutic relation, alterity relation, background relation, cyborg relation, immersion, augmentation.[26]

While Verbeek illustrates the application of mediation theory in the context of industrial design, the classification of mediation types lends itself particularly well to the context of interaction design in a hybrid city.

## STAGING THE ACTION

When attention shifts from the artifact and the technology per se toward a comprehensive consideration of interaction and activity, then the role that the artifact or system plays takes center stage—and here quite literally. In theater, such a role is played by a character. It requires a script. And that script is enacted on a stage.

Brenda Laurel's model that views *computers as theater*[27] expands the notion of interface from an entity that represents mental models of both user and machine to each other toward an emphasis on representing actions and activity. Theater is used as a model for the performance of intentional activity in which both human and computer have a role. They are concerned in representing whole actions, and these involve multiple agents. Laurel suggests "ways in which we can use a notion of theatre not simply as metaphor, but as a way to conceptualize human-computer interaction itself."[28]

Aristotle's *Rhetoric* and *Poetics* and their principles of well-formed speech and dramatic theater form the basis of Laurel's approach to using the structure of drama to design interactions between human and machine actors. Aristotle describes the poetic composition of ancient Greek drama as a logical process and conceptualizes four modes of causality in drama (formal, material, efficient, and final cause), as well as six foundational elements (action/plot, character, thought, language, melody/pattern, and spectacle/enactment). Using these foundational elements, Laurel develops a framework for human-computer interaction that views the designer and developer in the role of a director who facilitates the staging of whole actions and interactions by agents, considering a comprehensive spectrum of factors that mediate human experience.

The second framework that Laurel draws from is the dramatic structure articulated by the German novelist and playwright Gustav Freytag in his 1863 opus *Die Technik des Dramas*. Freytag analyzes ancient Greek and Shakespearean drama with the intent of understanding the structural format of dramatic action in these plays. As a result of his work, Freytag developed a graphical representation of the dramatic structure of theater in the form of what has become known as a "Freytag pyramid" or "Freytag triangle." It articulates a dramatic work as consisting of five parts: exposition, rising action, climax, falling action, and denouement.

Since Laurel's early work, drama-based design methods have more recently gained attention in the context of design related to *storytelling* and the practice of *storymapping*. The term *storymapping* appears to have been coined by Jeff Patton in a blog post in October 2008, after his introduction of related concepts without using the term as such in 2005.[29] Storymapping as presented by Patton did not make use of Freytag's pyramid and today is commonly referred to in terms of *experience mapping, customer journey diagram,* and *service blueprint*. These and similar notational methods have recently been critically discussed and summarized in clarifying and useful terms as *alignment diagrams* by the information and experience designer James Kalbach.[30]

The use of the term *storymapping* in more recent literature, however, has changed from being a method of mapping activities of people in relation to a product or a service—as is the case in the alignment diagrams—to becoming a method of constructing stories in which roles are constructed for users and consumers as well as for products and services.[31] The key idea of storymapping is to build products and systems as if they were stories themselves.

Storymapping uses story as a critical sense-making tool, arguing that if people experience something with a story at its foundation, they are more likely to "remember the experience, see value in what was experienced, see utility in what they did during that experience, have an easier time doing whatever they are trying to accomplish, [and] want to repeat that experience."[32]

The questions following this approach include "about what is the story?"; "who is the hero?"; and "what is the hero's goal?" And the response to these questions in the related literature appears to be, "Life is a story. And in that story, you are the hero."[33] Casting users as heroes of the story, the design task then becomes configuring a system that supports them in their journey, helping heroes overcome their challenges and obstacles and making progress toward their goals.

The storymapping method, as presented by Donna Lichaw, is based on the dramatic structure from Freytag's work, as introduced to the design context by Laurel's *Computers as Theatre*. In this structure, different types of stories are constructed for different moments of the human-product interaction, such as concept stories, origin stories, and usage stories. Storymapping is an interesting and effective design method, as it continues with the mission of shifting the focus away from technology features and toward activity. Lichaw, in fact, suggests, "create a successful product by mapping the story before you design or build anything."[34] Inasmuch as storymapping consists in constructing stories, it suggests the full-fledged construction of causal relationships between events and their consequences as well as impacts on the life of the story's agents.

Inevitably, the critical question that arises is *who* the author of these stories is. The strength and limitation of storymapping and the use of classical drama for design is that *there is an author* (in the form of the storymapping designer). The presence of an author makes the process of constructing stories manageable and compares operationally to how designers construct configurations of product features. In real life, however, following the philosopher Hannah Arendt, "the stories, the results of action and speech, reveal an agent, but this agent is not an author or producer. Somebody began it and is its subject in the twofold sense of the word, namely, its actor and sufferer, but nobody is its author."[35] Equally, in relation to the walkers of cities, de Certeau reminds us that they "compose a manifold story that has neither author nor spectator, shaped out of fragments of trajectories and alterations of spaces."[36] In the way that storymapping and the use of dramatic techniques necessitate an author, they are limited in their use as design methods by the very presence of that author-designer. The author is the original creator of the story and at the same time its limit, in that the author can only tell his or her story, and this becomes a limit when the audience of these stories is anything but passive spectators. The "distinction between a real story and a fictional story is that the latter is 'made up' while the former is not made at all," affirms Arendt; "real stories, in distinction from those we invent, have no author."[37]

The role of the *hero* is another element to consider closely in the use of drama for design. In storymapping, the hero is identified by the designer and constructed as someone who "overcomes challenges, surpasses obstacles, and makes progress towards goals."[38] Arendt contrasts this interpretation when she suggests that the hero, in its original meaning, needs no heroic qualities but is the person "about whom a story could be told." The heroic element, instead, comes into play through the "willingness to act and speak" as well as "to insert one's self into the world and begin a story of one's own."[39]

In this sense, a design in favor of heroes points to a design for *action* and *participation*. A design in favor of heroes is a design that points to a radical shift from the notion of user and consumer to one of *participant, citizen,* or, quite simply, *person.*

Laurel does contemplate that shifting relation between actor and spectator when noting the transformation of audience from passive observers to active participators.[40] What she does maintain from drama, however, is the script: the text that is at the basis of classical drama, which is written by an author, is written ahead of the enactment, and ensures that drama is quite unlike real life.

In that Freytag's five-part structure is based on classical drama lies its limitation for its use as a design method today. Fundamental to classic dramatic theater is the use of a script as a starting point. It mimics and imitates real life by constructing a fictional world characterized by a closed logic that operates within the play. Written by an author and produced by a director, classic drama is staged in a setting that includes a "fourth wall" that invisibly separates the actors and their actions from the observing audience.

The way in which we experience our world, however, tends to be far from being as causal and logical as it is presented in drama. In being so logical, dramatic theater falls short of truthfully mimicking our experience of the real world. The process of choice and decision-making takes place during rehearsal or practice and not during the actual staging of the performance. In the sense that drama formulates the enactment and not the action, it is unlike real life.

Instead, in improvisational techniques used during rehearsal, as in real life, anything can happen, actions are situated in context and always in flux, situations are essentially unique, and the focus is on dynamic choice in a dynamic environment. In theater, improvisation more closely mirrors the process of humans' interactions with their environment and, as such, points to a useful model for the design of interactions in today's urban context. The technologies that were previously contained in devices are embedded and mobile, networked, and ubiquitous in urban environments. Today, the interface as a theater that Laurel describes has left the confinement of both the digital screen and the formal space of the theater; it has spread out to become the city itself.

## THEATER BEYOND DRAMA

Theater has always reflected its historical, social, and cultural context. In order to leverage theater for the design process today, more than solely relying on forms from past centuries, a look at contemporary developments is necessary.

Developments in avant-garde theater since the late 1960s have been summarized under the notion of *postdramatic theater*. The term was coined by the theater scholar Hans-Thies Lehmann together with Andrzej Wirth in 1987 during their collaboration at the Institut für Angewandte Theaterwissenschaft in Gießen, Germany, which was founded by Wirth. The first German edition of the eponymous book by Lehmann was published in 1999, and it was followed by an English translation in 2006.[41] It has since become a key reference study.

The concept of postdramatic theater summarizes a diverse range of transformations that include different forms of performance, participatory theater, and improvisation. Despite the obvious diversity, these new forms of performance have one key characteristic in common: the dramatic text is no longer the necessary focus and starting point of the work.

Postdramatic theater is defined in opposition to dramatic theater, and the absence of the dramatic text as the sole reference opens up the possibility for other elements to become the starting point for a performance. Performances can have no plot at all, but, if a text is used, it is used in relation with the concrete material situation of the performance and the space where it is being performed, be that a stage or otherwise. The focus is on interactions among performers, audience, and place, with the objective of *producing an effect* among spectators who in postdramatic theater can also be participants.

Actual human experience is rarely as causal and logical as traditional fiction and dramatic theater would suggest. In this sense, dramatic forms of theater fail to mimic our actual experience of the real world. Postdramatic theater rejects simple logical causal sense being made from a piece of theater. Instead, it represents the world in its conflicting, contrasting, and irreconcilable multiple logics, maintaining simultaneous forms of perceiving situations from multiple perspectives. It preserves the ambiguity of a performance, which creates the space for personal interpretations.

The focus shifts from director-based acting toward performances based on collective forms of authorship through an engagement with the *real* of the situation, of the material and immaterial aspects of the setting. The *fourth wall,* the imagined wall along the proscenium that separates actors onstage from the audience in the auditorium, is broken down. The role of the audience changes from a passive spectator to that of an active participant that engages in the experience of the performance rather than solely observing a representation performed by actors.

Postdramatic theater emphasizes the unique process of performance creation in a particular space at a particular time and in context, rather than the staging of repetitions. It is focused on process and considers the organization of a performance holistically and as part of the work, including moments of preparation and experience of the action, reflection, and discussion of the happening among performers and audience.

In that postdramatic theater does away with a dramatic text as a basis, it is open to actions that emerge from the specific moment, that are unplanned, ad hoc, and improvised in the way in which they engage with the comprehensive performance and all of its components. Lehmann borrows from Erving Goffman the concept of a *social situation,* which the latter refers to as "the full spatial environment anywhere within which an entering person becomes a member of the gathering that is (or does then become) present. Situations begin when mutual monitoring occurs and lapse when the penultimate person has left."[42] Theater ceases to be only spectatorial and representational. The experience of participating in each and every performance is unique and distinct from that of others. The experience of the performance is constructed by participants as they are fully present at the event. They acknowledge the performance as much as the performance and performers acknowledge and work with the actual presence of the participants.

To my knowledge, there are only a few instances of work in the domain of design that explicitly engage with notions of postdramatic theater. The dramaturg Peter Sloth Madsen and the director Michael Spencer have collaborated with design professionals and companies using postdramatic theater techniques in design research investigating situations such as urban street crossings and social interactions in logistics warehouses.[43] Merja Ryöppy, Salu Ylirisku, Preben Friis, and Jacob Buur in their work deliberately move beyond scenario acting as the more common use of theater in interaction design, where it is used to evaluate new products and service offerings.[44] Using postdramatic theater, they introduce three formats of participant engagement for the process of designing for smart city contexts: multi-stakeholder theater, field study theater, and future product theater. The work with postdramatic theater allows them to overcome characteristics of traditional theater, such as the foundation of the dramatic text, the mimetic emphasis, and the exclusion of the real and the actual in a play. In their format "future product theater," for example, participants "confront product ideas early on with current practices of the prospective users" and "act out both the idea of an intelligent product and the users in order to imagine interactions between these two." Ryöppy et al. see the significance of postdramatic theater for design in its enabling participants to engage in a reflexive practice that sets the stage for "developing a shared experience of a future."[45] In this process, some participants act as users, while others act out the nonhuman machinery (such as the concept of a responsive bus stop in one of their examples). In doing so, they adopt a further trait from postdramatic theater: the animation and responsive use of inanimate things.

I suggest taking the work with postdramatic theater in the context of design yet a step further, as it would fall short if its forms and aesthetics were to be used with the end result of constructing once again a definite structure of a product or system. It would fall short were it to be employed in order to arrive at a fixed plan, a script. Instead, leveraging the essence of postdramatic theater opens up the possibility of conceiving of products and systems whose very role and performance in an everyday context can do without a script and can, instead, be based on improvisation. In this way, such structures would truly take on traits from postdramatic theater in their operation and in their behavior. Looking at postdramatic theater as a resource for design opens up a path for overcoming the plan- and script-based nature of the way we design artifacts and systems. It enables methods that embrace and constructively work with *uncertainty* and *unpredictability* as intrinsic characteristics of the actual everyday experience. Postdramatic theater does away with the script and puts the improvised act center stage. It creates an improvised act that is tightly intertwined with the social and material context of the performance and that transforms the performer-audience relationship. In performance terms, the spectator becomes a participant and a performer. In design terms, the user ceases to be a sole user or consumer and instead becomes a producer and co-creator that brings him- or herself into the action and that does so in unscripted ways. Now, the constructed world has to live up to a newly emancipated user-creator.

And for this, I suggest looking at the art and practice of improvisation, a core component of postdramatic theater, to inform the way we design the behavior of responsive urban environments. The aim is to develop a method of designing things so that they can go beyond their planned and programmed behavior, so that they are able to improvise, and so that they can facilitate improvised interactions with and between their human counterparts. By identifying the interactions in and with urban responsive environments and the art of improvisation as fundamentally related topics of investigation, I suggest we turn squarely toward improvisation for a more systematic understanding of responsive urban environments in the hybrid cities of today.

# 4 IMPROVISATION AS SYSTEM

When we think *improvisation,* we tend to think first of improvised music
or theater or dance; but beyond their own delights, such art forms are doors
into an experience that constitutes the whole of everyday life. We are all
improvisers. . . . Whether we are creating high art or a meal, we improvise
when we move with the flow of time and with our own evolving consciousness, rather than with a preordained script or recipe.

—STEPHEN NACHMANOVITCH, *Free Play*

## CITY STAGES FOR IMPROVISATION

A prominent historical example of the city as a place for improvisation is the *commedia dell'arte.* This form of theatrical
performance originated in cities of the then not yet unified Italian
peninsula in the sixteenth century. Commedia dell'arte was the first
form of professional actor group, a traveling business enterprise
that was, as a genus, "professional, masked and initially publicly
improvised on temporary outdoor platforms in simple costumes."[1]

Commedia dell'arte, also referred to as *commedia all'improviso
all'italiana,* was a major development in Italian Renaissance theater. It was different from other theater performances, as there
was no script. Commedia performances, instead, centered on
stock characters, their characteristic masks, and improvisation.
Actors would often be associated with their specific character for
many years (or even their entire career), and this level of lengthy
and intensive preparation was the basis for the often high levels
of improvisation in commedia performances.

The first account of a commedia dell'arte performance dates back to the mid-sixteenth century, and commedia remained a successful form of performance until the end of the following century.[2] Actor groups traveled throughout the Italian peninsula and other parts of Europe, in particular France, where commedia performances influenced, among others, the work of Molière. Commedia dell'arte was based on a schema or *scenario,* short notes and indications for the improvised play. These were written in such a way that left ample room for different interpretations, and, ultimately, everything was subject to the law of *all'improviso.*[3] Around eight hundred *scenari,* also known as *soggetti* or *canovacci,* are known from the seventeenth to eighteenth centuries. A particularly renowned example of these was *Il teatro delle favole rappresentative* by Flaminio Scala (Venice 1611).[4]

Commedia dell'arte performances were often staged outdoors on makeshift stages or (quite literally) in the streets, at market places and fairs.[5] This is also the way we often see them depicted in historical prints and paintings such as those by Peeter van Bredael (1629–1719). There appears to be some controversy about the significance of commedia as an outdoor form of theater. Judith Chaffee and Oliver Crick suggest that the commedia performances were not only staged outdoors and that the more accomplished groups aspired to and preferred to perform in indoor theaters, which provided better infrastructure and stage setups.[6] They argue that historical images depicting outdoor performances of commedia showcase less successful commedia groups, pointing to what might have been a constant struggle of more accomplished commedia performers to dissociate themselves from the stigma attached to street players and charlatans. "When members of a successful Commedia dell'Arte company were seen in a market square, it may have been because they were raising extra funds on the way to perform in another city, because they had been commissioned to perform there, or because they were giving a preview to entice audiences to a ticketed performance elsewhere."[7]

When trying to understand the role of indoor and outdoor locations for commedia performances, an additional dimension to consider is that of the limited availability of theater buildings at the time. The first account of a commedia performance dates back to 1568, while the construction of Italy's rich landscape of public theaters began only in the late sixteenth century and continued then during the seventeenth and eighteenth centuries. The Teatro Olimpico in Vicenza, for example, was built between 1580 and 1584, nearly twenty years after that first documented commedia dell'arte performance.

While the Teatro Olimpico is often referred to as the world's oldest enclosed theater, there appear to have been precursors to it. In 1499, for example, Ercole I d'Este began experimenting with scenography for Renaissance plays and converted the Sala Grande of his palace into a theater. Five years after that, in 1504, he began construction of the Sala delle Commedie, what would have been the first purpose-built theater since Roman times. D'Este died before the construction could be completed, and his family did not continue his project. Also, it is unclear whether that theater was intended to serve a private or public function. His son Alfonso d'Este does seem, however, to have helped convert an apothecary shop in the city of Ferrara into what appears to have become the first public theater space in the Italian peninsula, in 1531.[8]

The enclosed theater as we know it today was only at the beginning of its history when commedia dell'arte emerged as an art form. While more proficient and esteemed commedia groups probably aspired to stage their performances indoors at noble courts and better-equipped stage setups, it seems safe to say that public theaters were not as common a scene in Italian cities when the commedia was born as they were to become throughout the seventeenth and eighteenth centuries. Be it by choice or because of a lack of other accommodation, it does appear that there was a substantial performance activity of commedia dell'arte in public spaces. The sixteenth century saw urban dwellers from all parts of society come in close contact with commedia as an early form of theatrical improvisation in the very public realm of Italian cities.

In this way, either on modest platforms or directly on city squares, streets, or markets, commedia actors would do away with a script and improvise their performance. But why would actors improvise and forgo what would appear to be the safer way of reciting from script? The reasons appear to be manifold and of interest to considering improvisation for the design of interactions in today's urban context.

While a script casts the performance in one language and dialect, improvisation allowed the performance to be adapted on the fly to the then many local languages and dialects of the Italian peninsula without requiring a formal translation. As the story was improvised, it could be adapted up to the last minute to embrace current local events and the political situation—the *scenari* were of guidance but left room for such adaptations.

There was also another reason. The letters of church censors of the 1500s and 1600s complain that "it is impossible to censor them [the commedia dell'arte groups], because every show is different and they come up with the most unbelievable things to do that one would never think of, when you tell them not to do something."[9] By not tying performances to scripts that were defined and written prior to the act of performance, performers were less prone to political or religious censorship. They were, instead, free to tackle topics and issues in opposition to the desires of the throne and church order. Performances happened on the spot and in the moment, defying the operations of censorship, which depended on premeditated plans and action.

This subversive nature of acting-in-the-moment is also what Michel de Certeau discusses four centuries later in *The Practice of Everyday Life*. He focuses on the innumerable "ways of operating," the everyday tactics, by means of which users reappropriate space organized by powerful strategies and techniques of sociocultural production. De Certeau looks at how people take shortcuts between formally proposed paths, what people actually do with systems put in place for them to consume, and what clandestine forms of practice and procedure of everyday interactions exist relative to structures of expectation, negotiation, and improvisation.[10]

The focus on control in much of the work with networked urban information systems today—such as the aforementioned urban control centers—diverts from the value found in dynamics that lie outside one's control. What is beyond control is also beyond expectation, and that has always been one of the fascinating attractions of cities: to move to places where something that is beyond what could be expected can indeed happen.

## ON THE NATURE OF IMPROVISATION

To work productively with what is beyond control and beyond expectation is precisely the essence of improvisation. The word's very etymology indicates a form of acting without prior agreement, an acting that is not based on a previously developed plan that is to be executed but that is, instead, formed and informed by the contingencies of the moment and the context of action.

In the performing arts, the practice of improvisation has been studied and experimented with extensively. Jazz is one of the domains intensively invested in this phenomenon, and the development of free jazz in the 1950s and 1960s led to exhaustive experiments of composing in real time.[11] In this context and in that of music in a broader sense, improvisation is a process in which conception and execution collapse into a single moment: they happen simultaneously. It is composing while playing, wherein what is being played and the circumstances under which it is being played continuously feed back into the process of composition.

In this sense, the perspective of improvisation that I espouse in this book differs from the way in which improvisation is frequently considered a lesser form of acting, motivated by necessity and by the lack or absence of a script, program, or plan.[12] Improvisation is often considered a stopgap modality of getting by until things work again according to plan or program. When I describe improvisation as a form of critical mobility, I mean, instead, an attitude of readiness to shift, to move beyond any previously planned courses of action and, instead, to base next steps on an attention to an in-the-moment evaluation of the actual situation at hand.

One of the enigmas that surround improvisation is the question of where an unprecedented, unplanned act originates. When someone or something acts following a program or plan, the action is seen as a consequence of that plan. Where, instead, does an improvised act originate? One answer to this points toward the consideration of improvisation as a system that relates the moment of action beyond its temporal focus on the here and now.

While improvisation is an acting in the moment, the circumstances of the moment are not the sole source of action. Improvisation may not be preceded by a plan, but it is preceded by past experience and processes of preparation. Performers invest extensive time and energy in the practice of their art. In their practice they develop their technique but also their attention to and awareness of their acting and their interactions with factors external to themselves. When performers improvise, they draw from these processes of preparation and from material generated during their practice. Instead of repeating this material during their performance, they elaborate it in relation to the specific conditions and circumstances of the moment and ideas that emerge from it and from their interaction with it. In this way, variations are created and new features are added every time.[13] To talk about improvisation also means to consider the notion of inventiveness in a way that involves elements of both novelty and repetition of past patterns in a broader context. The debate on the possibility or impossibility of true originality is long standing. In Kant, the definition of a genius is one who is capable of the utmost original act, free from all that was before, disrupting any previous convention or norm.[14] Jacques Derrida, on the other hand, talks about the impossibility of total originality due to an ever present repetition of the past.[15] In practice, the improvised act is likely to be found somewhere between these two antipodes, involving both elements of novelty and repetition of past patterns. While not following a previously formulated plan as such, improvisation does acquire in this way some form of consistency, in that it connects with what has come before in an ongoing process of repetition and variation.[16] Each performance is distinct from all others,[17] and we can "conceive of improvisation as an iterative and recursively operating process where dynamic structures emerge from the processing and reprocessing of elements."[18] With this understanding, we capture more of the essence of the practice, which enables us to identify structures in a process that can, at first, appear ephemeral. Improvisation moves beyond mutually exclusive opposites such as repetition and novelty, security and risk, order and disorder, information and noise. Such opposites are equally embraced and constitute the very nature of the improvised act, which is characterized by complexity and multiplicity rather than by binary distinctions.[19]

The phenomenology of the moment for improvisational performers is as much material for their art as is their past training and practice of structures and procedures. In ensemble work, each performer feeds off and builds on what others do. As the performers interact with each other, they pass cues back and forth, consciously or unconsciously. They are perceived and interpreted, and it matters less whether they are interpreted in the intended way. They become part of a collective creation of meaning that informs the interaction. Improvisational performers not only pick up on gestures, sequences played and acted by their fellow performers, but also develop a capability to recognize form when it is in the making, attributing meaning to the completed form of which they see the seed—they feed forward. The attributed meaning and the action based on it become the novel element that an actor contributes to the collective process regardless of whether the original action was executed toward that expectation. Misunderstandings and errors are constructive elements in improvisation. They are the noise that leads to the emergence of new structures.

The meaning of an action in improvisation lacks stability over time, as every act by one performer is capable of altering the meaning of any previous act. As such, meaning is not defined by any one action in a definitive and determinate way, but rather each act contributes to what is ultimately a recursive process that defines itself and in which the authorship lies in the process of actions and interactions rather than in any one subject or its contribution. It is that recursive and iterative nature of improvisation and its emergent character that constitutes improvisation as a system.

New structures emerge from nonsimple interactions between many different parts that interact in parallel, forming a complex system. This resulting system is self-organizing and complicates boundaries between interiority and exteriority. It is a system that is neither fixed nor static but that evolves and adapts.[20] Adapting a systems view of improvisation makes the tension between the notions of stability and variation a productive one.

Parallels are often drawn between the way actors or musicians improvise and the phenomenology of spoken language, of discourse and conversations. "It's like language: you're talking, you're speaking, you're responding to yourself. When I play, it's like having a conversation with myself."[21] Rather than telling a story, those who are improvising *are* the story. They are participating observers that make and form the story as much as they are a product of that same story.

Also in the context of systems theory, the interactions between the constituent parts of a system and between systems are likened to the process of a conversation. The cybernetician Gordon Pask discusses how "structures may be designed (as well as intuited) to foster a productive and pleasurable dialogue."[22]

Conversational processes between humans and their environment, as discussed by Pask, and the process of improvisation, as just described, share a fundamental characteristic: they both build on elements that are present prior to the action. These elements can be structural elements or procedural sequences. Actions from past experiences are iterated under an astute awareness for the special circumstances (internal and external) of a unique situation, leading to variations in the repetition. New features emerge and are added to those that came before, and the systems involved (both human and machine) change, adapt, and evolve; they *learn*.

Improvisation in the performing arts has advanced to a high level both in practice and in theoretical frameworks. Techniques and training methods have been formalized that provide a detailed and structured understanding of the learning process to develop the capabilities to improvise. It is on these premises that I propose to look at improvisation as a mind-set well indicated to inform the design of responsive and interactive environments in the context of today's cities.

## DIMENSIONS OF IMPROVISATION

With this expanded view of improvisation, I want to highlight four key dimensions that emerge as particularly significant to improvisation and to the work with improvisation in the context of design for urban interactions.

### Beginnings

Etymologically, *improvisation* refers to actions taken in absence of a provision, of an agreement or a plan, and deals with the unforeseen and unexpected. How, then, does improvisation begin? A critical aspect of any improvisation is precisely this: the beginning. In the absence of prior coordination and agreement, how and when does someone or something begin an action? In improvisation, the beginning of an action can be born solely out of context and out of an agent's initiative.

Taking initiative is deeply ingrained in human nature. Hannah Arendt in *Vita Activa* argues that "to act, in its most general sense, means to take initiative, to begin (from the Greek *archein*, meaning 'to begin,' 'to lead,' 'to rule'), to set something in motion (which is the original meaning of the Latin *agere*)."[23] It is in the nature of beginning that something new is started that cannot be expected from whatever may have happened before. "This character of startling unexpectedness is inherent in all beginnings and in all origins. . . . The new always happens against the overwhelming odds of statistical laws and their probability. . . . The fact that man is capable of action means that the unexpected can be expected from him, that he is able to perform what is infinitely improbable."[24] Embracing this profound reflection today means also to look critically at the planning paradigm of probability-based predictive modeling. Today's availability of massive amounts of data generated by systems of telecommunication, transportation, health care, and the like, which is incidental to everyday human activity, is often used as an undisputed basis for the planning and implementation of systems that become based on the past and on probable futures. Instead, I suggest that the hybrid city, with its pervasive networks of connected devices and digital-physical interfaces, need not be limited to this. Quite on the contrary, a value of these technologies lies in the ability to facilitate and support ad hoc behavior and interactions, a decision forming and acting in response to the moment and to a given situation—a move from probability to possibility.

## Openness

Besides initiative, improvisation is born out of context. The degree of openness toward this context is paramount, as the situation in the moment continues to feed into what is being done.

Improvisation is, however, not so much about creating or maintaining any one particular work but rather about ensuring an openness toward a process of ongoing creation. Initiative is not reduced to a singular moment but pervades improvisation in its entirety. Improvisation is an ongoing taking of initiative; it is a behavioral space that is open to continuously taking a first step.

Gary Peters discusses this condition in reference to Heidegger's description of the existential triangular relation between the artist, the artwork, and the art: the artist makes the artwork, but also the artwork, once conceived, makes the artist, as there can be no artist without the artwork created by the artist. Furthermore, both artwork and artist only exist in virtue of such a prior notion of art, giving way to a tight interdependence between these three notions. This existential interdependence ensures that the creative act is not a single act but the beginning of a process that ties the artist to the working of the work rather than to any one particular piece of art that may be generated as an outcome.[25]

If we apply this perspective to improvisation, it becomes clear that keeping the improvisation going upstages any structure that might emerge during the process. Whatever physical, behavioral, or social structure emerges from an improvised interaction is only secondary to the primary goal of maintaining a condition of openness that allows for new structures to be formed as well as taken apart.

In this perspective, what becomes a principal focus for the design of responsive systems in hybrid cities is the fostering of openings for human initiative—creating an artifact, a system, or modalities of interaction that continue to invite new interactions. Systems that espouse this notion of openness will be open to an extent that human initiative can generate variations that are significant enough to become foundational for the process of interaction itself.

### Time

Practitioners of improvisation describe time as paramount in their work. Kent De Spain's book *Landscape of the Now* is based on a series of interviews conducted with eight esteemed practitioners and teachers of movement improvisation.[26] In their discussions about time, the performers share their exploration of conceptions of time that are different from the more conventional notions of clock time.

Anna Halprin distinguishes *site time* from *body time*. The site time she discusses is specific to place, to seasons, to time of day, and to culture. Body time, instead, comes from a person's uniqueness of breath and pulse. She explores the upbeats of inhale and the downbeats of exhale and how they interact with gravity.

For De Spain, "time is the somatic experience of change," and thus the very bodily experience of change is in contrast to a cognitive understanding.[27] How do our senses register change? Lisa Nelson reminds us that different senses measure time differently, and therefore perception itself cannot do away with considering time. Nancy Stark Smith explores time in her work through the shifting of awareness and the effect of this shifting on how we act. "A shift in awareness changes your relationship to the moment and, therefore, what you do in that moment. You don't have to *make* something happen."[28]

As a consequence, time can be the key and a tool to opening up awareness, even through prosaic interventions such as speeding up or slowing down an activity or a gesture. "By taking everyday movements and altering their rhythms, their speeds, their time harmonics, we can crack open the unconscious portion of the template process. We can become fully aware (as fully as we are capable) of things for the first time since we awkwardly struggled to learn them in the first place."[29]

Shifting awareness of time, then, can be as easy as turning your attention toward it, but how are we sensing time, or in De Spain's terms, "what part of your somatic experience is engaging with *change*?"[30]

In Viewpoints improvisation, four of the nine viewpoints are dedicated to time.[31] Experimenting with the viewpoint *tempo* explores slowing down or speeding up; the viewpoint *duration* explores what is too short to start something and what is too long for something to die. Time is personal, but it is also cultural and universal; and shifting awareness can create the possibility of what De Spain refers to as *performance time*—a playing with time, molding time, laughing at time, and literally *taking* your time.[32] This provides a way to contrast the inevitable march of clock time.

If time relates to an experience of change, then timing is related to our expectations. Timing is described by performers as something that "does magic," and it does this magic because it intervenes in our expectations. We expect things to happen in a way that is similar to our past experience, in a way that we know or that we believe to know. We have experienced things to work in certain ways. We expect them to work in certain ways because of these experiences. "Altering the rhythm, the timing, of certain moments can snap us back to attention."[33]

Improvisation as a mode of operation that does away with a plan or script formulated up front makes moments of conception and execution coincide. And this opens up the possibility to intervene in our expectations at any point. It opens up the possibility of shifting awareness and thus of manipulating the very way we feel time.

Time, in this perspective, is closely related to our senses. And this makes it interesting when considering networked embedded technologies capable of altering physical configurations or aesthetic qualities of environments.

## Otherness

Improvisation opens a space in the here and now for an act that comes unannounced, that comes about by a conversion of elements, some of which are present only in that moment. The simultaneity of conception and action bestows on the improvised act its quality of unpredictability. It plays with our expectations that are based on past experiences. Will a gesture seen before follow the known path, or will it diverge? The moment in the act surprises. It surprises even the performer him- or herself since the meaning of that act emerges from an interaction between that moment and those that came before and those that will follow. The meaning of a gesture of an act comes from the intentionality of the actor, but any successive act by another actor can and will more or less radically alter that meaning. Improvisation is interaction with others. These others can be humans, they can be artifacts, or they can also be characteristics of the moment or elements of memory. The meaning of the improvised act is constructed and reconstructed in recursive iterations, and, as such, they can have no single author. The story of the improvisation, rather, is constructed by the sum of its interactions and can be *read* only in hindsight.

As part of this dynamic, improvisation is particularly characterized by the fact that at any moment something *other* than the expected can happen. This is due to the absence of a plan in improvisation. There is also no guarantee for any performer and any one act to maintain its intended meaning at the moment of the act. Something other may come from it once the act has been performed. Improvisation lives from allowing this kind of otherness and by embracing this emergent otherness as critical mobility.

The otherness that improvisation involves and allows for cannot be anticipated by considering any one actor's own range of actions. It is more akin to Lacan's capital-*O Other*, the provocative, perturbing, disturbing enigma of the Other as an unknowable. It is different from Lacan's lowercase-*o other*, which is used when referring to the other as an alter-ego, someone or something thought of as being akin to or like oneself.

Folding the rich art and practice of improvisation into the way we look at the design of interactions in today's hybrid urban environments means allowing for this Otherness. It means allowing for the unexpected and the unforeseeable, embracing this Other in the way we shape and activate our environment.

## UNPREDICTABILITY AS CRITICAL MOBILITY

Bringing essential elements of improvisation to the very way we understand and design for interaction leverages some key attributes of the improvised act that I believe are of value to the condition of today's hybrid city and that merit being made explicit. Designing for improvisation means inherently designing for *adaptability, resilience,* and *participation* as well as *agency*. It embraces an approach to design built on *surprise* and even *shock,* and by the nature of its operation, it is in continuous quest for *relevance* in a continuously changing context.

### Adaptability and Resilience

To improvise is to engage with the unforeseen, that which could not be predicted and expected. It is engaging with something that happens out of the ordinary and that takes us by surprise. Improvisation is a working with this unexpectedness in constructive terms. The unexpected becomes a part of the solution, becomes part of the way forward rather than something to be avoided, rejected, ignored, or feared. The unexpected becomes the opportunity; it is necessary to move forward. There is no improvisation without unexpected elements. Improvisation seeks the unexpected to evolve, to progress, and to develop.

This working with the unexpected is an existential trait of improvisation. To improvise means to adapt in one way or another to unexpected events. Adaptation can comprise an adjustment of one's action in light of the unexpected event or to change the goal or intention. Adaptation can bring about a more or less radical change from the formerly intended course of action.

Because improvisation is so deeply and fundamentally connected with dealing constructively with the unexpected, it is closely related to dynamics of resilience. Resilience describes a capacity to recover from difficulties, an ability of a system to positively deal with change. In ecology, resilience describes "the capacity of a system to absorb disturbance and reorganize while undergoing change so as to still retain essentially the same function, structure, identity, and feedbacks."[34] In the context of organizational studies, the British BSI Standard defines organizational resilience as the "ability to anticipate, prepare for, respond and adapt to events—both sudden shocks and gradual change."[35]

Since disturbances and sudden shocks in any context defy prediction, dealing with them in a way to "retain essentially the same function, structure, identity, and feedbacks" requires interacting with them, working with them in a way that goes beyond processes of a priori planning—neither of the two definitions mention the word *plan*. To plan means to anticipate a course of action and is a workable approach for action when events are predictable. When, as in real life, events are unpredictable—and often events that provide the most impactful disturbance come unexpectedly—following a preplanned course of action becomes problematic. *Preparation*, instead, consists in honing a set of capabilities that can be readily adjusted, reconfigured, and applied to any situation that may arise.

An example from the world of sports illustrates this idea well: training programs for marathon runners do not typically involve running an actual marathon distance before the race. They expose the athlete to a staged series of workouts that prepare for the event, that build resilience for the multiple and unpredictable challenges a runner will face when taking on the full marathon distance on the day of the event. These challenges include a runner's condition of health and motivation, as well as external climatic and environmental conditions. It is preparation more than repeatable planning that guides marathon runners in dealing with the unpredictability of the event.

Improvisation combines preparation and acting in the moment to constructively encounter unexpected events, disruptions, disturbances, and shocks. It is a resilience-based mind-set to deal well with setbacks by embracing them as constructive elements for moving forward.

## Participation

In an improvisation-based interaction, any participant can bring him- or herself into the action at any moment and unannounced. The action of any participant can become part of the performance, and, even more, anyone or anything can choose to become a participant. The openness of an improvisation includes not-yet participants. Anyone can inject him- or herself into an improvisation-based interaction and become part of the performance. There are no preassigned roles. Roles are fluid, and they are constructed and deconstructed in the moment of performance. No one is a priori part or not part of the performance. In fact, a participant is only part of the performance through his or her participation rather than by merely being there. Improvisation requires participation, and participation is the gateway to improvisation. The single act of a person becomes the unexpected contribution to the performance; it is this contribution, this gift, that makes one a performer.

In improvisation, the stakes are low, in that any act, any gesture, or any move can be an act of participation. Every act has a place; every act is authorized and legitimate. At the same time, the stakes in improvisation are high, in that no one has a place in the performance by default. To take part in the performance means to participate, to take a step and contribute a gesture without plan, and to take on a part in the performance.

## Agency

Designing any artifact or system is also a process of defining the possibilities for what can be done with it. A chair affords the possibilities to be sat on, to be moved around, or perhaps to be stacked. A park bench is probably fixed to the ground and so can be sat on but not moved; thus, the position is determined by the designer or planner and not by the person who encounters the bench as part of a walk in the park and wants to enjoy a seated repose. The user of a 311 online civic notification service can signal an issue or a complaint and can file it typically under one of a set of categories but cannot create a new category of issues. The set of categories is prescribed by the system planners and designers and in this case not by the citizen who uses the system. Current public bike-sharing systems have seen widespread adoption and reliable operation once the systems began to be tied to users' credit cards, which ensures a safety deposit in case of damage or theft. This enables someone in possession of a credit card to access this service but shuts out others. These are but a few brief examples to illustrate that the way products and systems are designed defines substantially how agency is distributed across a network of elements and participants.[36]

Improvisation is fundamentally based on a mind-set of shared and distributed agency. It is an open invitation to take action, to intervene, to do, to speak up, and to step in. Everyone can have a voice and a space to act. Improvisation not only tolerates action but requires action. An artifact, system, or service that is based on a mind-set of improvisation is one that actively invites and promotes the taking of action by a wide range of possible participants. It is open for participants to intervene in its content and structure, its form and behavior. It can also be thought of as taking action by itself, speaking up, and bringing itself into a dynamic in which it finds itself.

## Surprise and Shock

Back when I was in design school, an instructor used to point to the Kinder Surprise chocolate egg as an ideal combination of qualities in a product: a sensory pleasure (when eating the chocolate egg), an experience of delightful surprise (discovering the toy components inside the chocolate egg), and something to build yourself (constructing the toy from the included parts).[37] Besides these undebatable qualities of the Surprise eggs, the construction kits inside have also often served as a case study in design engineering classes due to their often-sophisticated techniques of injection molding. It is the moment of surprise, however, that I want to draw our attention to.

Improvisations take us by surprise in that they represent an unexpected event in the flow of a situation. They shock us, stand out, and strike us as unusual. Improvised acts are a surprise on their own, and they are a surprise by way of the relations that emerge through the sequence of actions and responses over time. Any one action might have its meaning changed by the next action by another actor. In this sea of unplanned actions, however, moments of coherence emerge. Musicians or actors play into the tune laid out by the previous acts. A musical theme is repeated or extended; a gesture is completed or responded to. At any moment, though, an action may disrupt that convergence of meaning and lead elsewhere.

The theater scholar Hans-Thies Lehmann points to the idea of shock as a fundamental motif in contemporary theater. In referring to Walter Benjamin, Karl Heinz Bohrer, Theodor Adorno, and Heiner Müller, Lehmann describes the shock in theater as an opening for new experience: "we must recognize the structure of a shock . . . by the experience of being startled when we suddenly realize we are missing something . . .—a signal we cannot interpret but that nevertheless affects us."[38] It is in this experience of lack of understanding when shocked that we can assist the appearance of something authentically new.

Lehmann equates this element of shock, of startling in theater, to an aesthetic of responsibility, in that the performance through its effect of shock addresses itself to the spectator's direct involvement: the shock of the appearance of something fundamentally new points to "my personal responsibility to realize the mental synthesis of the event; my attention having to remain open to what does not become an object of understanding; my sense of participation in what is happening around me; my awareness of the problematic act of spectating itself."[39]

Consisting in such a series of shocks, improvisation-based interaction does become the aesthetic of responsibility that Lehmann refers to. Meaning is not given with the action but requires a personal response, through attention and participation. As part of this process, an unprecedented understanding can be formed. Openings for individual and personal appropriations of moments appear by creating meaning in the instant of the event.

## RELEVANCE

Whatever it is that a designer designs, what performance a theater director directs, what musical piece a composer composes, a question that always arises is that about the relevance of the work. Relevance is an elusive concept that operates in relational terms. At a high level, it describes the quality of connectedness of one element to a second element with regard to how much the first element can contribute to the objective related to the second element. As an example, if the first element is evidence and the second element is theory, the first element can be of relevance to the second element if it supports or challenges that theory. The first element will be of no relevance if it does neither to the theory.

In interactions with our constructed world, an artifact is more or less relevant to someone if, in any given situation, the thing and its characteristics relate to the person's goals or objectives. More broadly, the artifact becomes more relevant if the artifact in any way gains the person's awareness, attention, or action, becoming part of a personal experience.

How, then, does relevance relate to improvisation? Think of this: during a theater play, the audience walks out of the performance in protest while the actors carry on their performance as if nothing happened, following the script as planned. The relevance of the performance itself after that point comes into question, the relevant event having become the event of the audience leaving the theater and to which the performers did not respond. Improvisation, instead, by acting in response to the moment and through heightened awareness and attention to context and situation, has an intrinsic ability to continuously relate to a dynamic situation, to remake itself relevant to the situation of which it is an integral part. Improvisation as a mode of interaction is a way to ensure relevance, in that every action springs from the situation and from

the moment, from the ongoing interaction between all participants. Improvisation adapts and adjusts. It changes the situation,
and it is changed by the situation. It mutates and evolves gradually as well as radically. As long as there is improvisation, acts
remain relevant. Improvisation is a mode of operation to remain
relevant, to ensure that one's actions will be relevant.

Design guided by an improvisation-based perspective on interaction, then, ensures that responsive systems and environments
are capable of working with unexpected situations in a way to
remain relevant in a continuously changing context.

## THE TURN TO PERFORMANCE

In the arts, the *performative turn* has brought attention to the
performance as an event in time and place, shared by performers
and audience as a unique experience, away from traditional venues such as theaters or museums, and liberated from cultural
norms that typically underlie performances there. Emphasis is
put on the act in the moment and in context. The social sciences
have since experienced their own performative turn, viewing
culture not as something that can be read like a text but rather as
something that is performed in the moment and in context. Goffman emphasizes the tight relation between social life and performance, examining the theater of performance in the panorama
of everyday public acts.[40] The performative turn in architecture
has been described by the architects Branko Kolarevic and Ali
Malkawi, among others, and by the architectural curator Pedro
Gadanho, who notes that the "return to the needs of the end-user
of architecture now takes place integrating use narratives into
conceptual strategies of design, but also by introducing expressions of these concerns into the very shaping of built forms."[41]

Design had its own performative turn with the emergence of
interaction design. "In the past, those who built interactive systems
tended to focus on the technology that makes them possible
rather than on the interfaces that allow people to use them. But
a system isn't complete without the people who use it. Like it or
not, people—irritable, demanding, and often distracted people

like ourselves—and their goals are the point of our systems, and we must design for them."[42] Furthermore, in the context of design, we may trace the roots of a turn to the performative as far back as to the Bauhaus theater productions by Oskar Schlemmer in the 1920s.

Long before the advent of ubiquitous networked technologies, aspects of openness and underspecification, of responsiveness to situations and context, have been explored; an emphasis on performance occurs around the 1960s. The "decade of interactive and adaptive architecture" was inspired by the concurrent explorations in interactive art, and, even if not referring to the term explicitly, several architects worked with key elements of improvisation.[43]

The Dutch painter and sculptor Constant Nieuwenhuys in 1956 began work on his seminal New Babylon project, which he then continued, with interruptions, until 1974. Constant was in contact with the Situationist International (SI) movement and its founder, Guy Debord, and also joined the movement for some time.

New Babylon is an "imaginary city," "not a town-planning project, but rather a way of thinking, of imagining, of looking at things and at life," in which residents and passers-through are freed from both "labor and hunger" by automation and experience new forms of freedom of movement, of expression, of social engagement, and of creative action.[44]

"The future constructions we envisage will need to be extremely supple in order to respond to a dynamic conception of life, which means creating our own surroundings in direct relation to incessantly changing ways of behavior."[45] The new *homo ludens* that will occupy New Babylon "will be able to circulate, to change his environment, to enlarge his area. His relationship to space will become as free as his relationship to time is already becoming now."[46]

"The different floors will be divided into neighboring and communicating spaces, artificially conditioned, which will offer the possibility of creating an infinite variety of ambiences, facilitating the dérive of the inhabitants and their frequent chance encounters. The ambiences will be regularly and consciously changed, with the aid of every technical means, by teams of specialized creators who will therefore be professional situationists."[47] Constant envisions constructed environments that are essentially responsive, in that their characteristics and behavior can adapt and can be adapted to the situations that people will actively create in them. While technologies play a role in these dynamics of adaptation, it is of interest that Constant identifies a role for humans to act as situationists who would change the environment through their direct intervention in an ad hoc and improvised manner.

When Constant writes of "professional situationists" that change ambience, Gordon Pask's work and involvement in Cedric Price's Fun Palace come to mind. The Fun Palace was conceived in the early 1960s as a reconfigurable adaptive space that could support a broad variety of activities that changed over time. The initiator of the project, the theater director Joan Littlewood, "turned . . . to a childhood dream of a people's palace, a university of the streets, re-inventing Vauxhall Gardens, the eighteenth-century Thames-side entertainment promenade, with music, lectures, plays, restaurants under an all-weather-dome."[48] The project was intended to offer a nonprescriptive space that not only could be adaptable to the varying activities staged in it but also would encourage ideas to grow and develop. Gordon Pask, the cybernetician, was involved by Price and Littlewood as the third key person in the project and organized the Fun Palace Cybernetics Subcommittee. His contribution to the Fun Palace followed his work on the MusiColour Machine, and he oversaw the modalities by which the Fun Palace would become an underspecified but highly responsive place. Constructed in 1953, MusiColour "was a performance system of colored lights that illuminated in concert with audio input from a human performer . . . in such a way that it becomes another performer in a performance, creating a unique (though non-random) output with every iteration."[49] The machine does not simply map predefined output patterns to detected input but varies its response on the basis of a number of factors that make its behavior unique at every instance. "It listens for certain frequencies, responds and then gets bored and listens elsewhere, produces as well as stimulates improvisation, and reassembles its language much like a jazz musician might in conversation with other band members."[50]

The behavior of a machine like MusiColour withstands any notion of "optimal" or "efficient" behavior. Instead, its behavior is continuously negotiated between the participant performer and the machine's sensitivities. It is the input of the human interacting with the machine that is used to generate behavior, yet the human cannot control the behavior of the machine as such.

In 1969, Pask wrote about the shift in view from a concept of a house as a "machine for living in" toward the "concept of an environment with which the inhabitant cooperates and in which he can externalize his mental processes, i.e. mutualism will be emphasized as compared with mere functionalism."[51] While never built, the Fun Palace continues to serve as an inspiring model for a constructed environment capable of facilitating active participation by its visitors and residents in shaping the very building, which in turn conditions people's own use of it in a constant back-and-forth.

The radical concept of Walking City by Archigram's Ron Herron from 1964 envisaged provocatively a city capable of walking as well as adapting to changes it encounters. The proposal, consisting of giant roaming pods that house public and residential areas, was part of a vision of a new architecture centered on circulation instead of statics and permanence. Herron was a founding member of the British collective Archigram, along with Peter Cook, whose Plug-In City from the same year (and mentioned earlier in this book) proposed to do away with buildings and instead offered a gigantic framework into which functional cells could be slotted according to changing needs and requirements.

In Italy, Andrea Branzi founded the avant-garde group Archizoom in 1966 together with Gilberto Corretti, Paolo Deganello, and Massimo Morozzi. Like Archigram and other radical architecture groups in the 1960s, Archizoom's work was a reaction against modernist architecture, downplaying practical issues and focusing on an imaginative and provocative outlook on architecture's role for society. Branzi's No-Stop City from 1969 is a vision for a city that offers an infinitely extensible, undistinguished indoor and outdoor space where individuals are able to engage firsthand in building their own forms of dwellings. In this way, the inhabitants of No-Stop City create new typologies of dwelling formats with a focus on openness, exploring new ways of gathering and constellations of community as the city evolves. The proposal was a radical new model of an immaterial city dedicated to flows of people, information, technical networks, services, and markets, where architecture in its traditional form disappears behind the emphasis on *performance*.

More recently, Jordan Geiger's *Entr'acte: Performing Publics, Pervasive Media, and Architecture* brings the discourses of architecture and urban space (and especially digitally networked space) into conversation with cultural and performance theory. Geiger's edited volume proposes the *entr'acte*, the *intermezzo* or *Zwischenspiel*, as a conceptual construct and a metaphor in relation to elements of linkages and gaps in digitally networked cities. Geiger stresses how "in today's public space formations, roles of new technologies are both prominent and noticeably time sensitive. Communications media change rapidly, practices of urban space use and uses of technology change rapidly, yet physical construction or urban spaces change relatively slower. . . . The entr'acte is an apt model for analyzing and synthesizing—*creating*—new forms and durations of public space."[52]

The work with *lack* in architecture is described by Omar Khan as a strategy that anticipates the inclusion of crowds (of people) for completion. Khan examines the "evolution of the crowd—from the senseless mob, to the animated crowd, to the wise collective— and how architecture and urbanism have accommodated it."[53] This is a look at the crowd as a key element used by architects in the creation of space. An element that is unpredictable but seductive emerges from Elias Canetti's descriptions of the moving and open crowds.[54] The lack is also a key characteristic in Lehmann's postdramatic theater and its focus on the production of presence. The presence that is coproduced between performers and an active audience is "an experience of emptiness," an "experience of lack or of having missed something,"[55] and requires filling through active part taking. Lack is present in the work of architects throughout history, from Constant's and Archizoom's work, mentioned earlier, to designs by Rem Koolhaas and the Office for Metropolitan Architecture (OMA) and Bernard Tschumi's Parc de la Villette, as well as work by Anne Lacaton and Jean-Philippe Vassal. The design itself seems to become a backdrop for crowd choreographies that fill the lack, such as those orchestrated by urban games based on digital maps on players' mobile devices. The lack identified by Khan is a kind of openness, with a structural vitality authored by the architect as a director and producer of the space that both frames the movement of the crowd and at the same time remains open to the surprise of how crowds will actualize.

In the context of urban planning, a direct use of principles from improvisation is presented by David Brown's Available City.[56] The project is "an ongoing speculative design that leverages the City of Chicago's ownership of 15,000 vacant lots to structure an improvisational production of a new public space system."[57] Organizational ideas come from different techniques of musical improvisation that inform the Available City initiative, which involves viewing vacant city-owned lots in Chicago as "catalyzing agents." The project proposes an intricate set of rules to enable private developers to extend their intervention beyond any one private lot but to include up to five lots that do not need to be adjacent. Developers can develop these lots vertically as long as space accessible to the public remains of equal surface area as the original public lots. The Available City, in this way, is not an a priori plan but an introduction of new relationships that transform public space from an entity that is given into one that is dynamically generated as a result of these improvisations. With such a set of rules and relational terms, "design as improvisation proposes to read design as continual redesign," in Christopher Dell and Ton Matton's analysis. They conceptualize the notion of improvisation technology, in which the contemporary city is considered a space of transition and where "transformations that arise from unexpected reactions and spontaneous productions of urban life nurture new forms of organization."[58] More specifically, in relation to urban infrastructure governance, Dietmar Offenhuber and Katja Schechtner carried out ethnographic research in Paco, Manila, in regard to social practices surrounding the provision and modernization of streetlights and electricity through formal and informal actors. On the basis of this work, they developed the notion of "improstructure" as a conceptual model for understanding infrastructure governance as an improvisational process of "call and response" among a diverse set of actors.[59]

The intersection of interactive art and developments related to what is summarized as artificial intelligence is another area in which the work with interactive environments encounters notions of improvisation. Simon Penny provides a brief historical overview of interactive art in his article "Improvisation and Interaction, Canons and Rules, Emergence and Play" and examines how the field of artificial intelligence has looked to improvisation for guidance for the design of computational artifacts that have behavior.[60] Penny discusses one of the key challenges in the attempt to develop human-like computational systems: the ability to display the same kind of agency as is typical of humans. This issue is also addressed by Omar Al Faleh, Nikolaos Chandolias, and Del Tredici Felix in their exploration of improvisational and performative interactive environments that allow participants to improvise with and within them.[61]

This *turn to performance* in a number of design- and planning-related domains has brought attention to improvised performance in new ways. By providing an understanding of the nature of improvisation, some of its key characteristics, and its historical ties with the urban context, this chapter provides a basis for the work with improvisation for the design in a hybrid city context. The radical and experimental work from the 1960s has gained new significance today, and networked information technologies have reached levels of performance and pervasiveness that were unthinkable half a century ago. Past works have used improvisation predominantly as a concept and metaphor. I suggest, instead, that we consider improvisation more thoroughly to inform a method for the design of interactions in hybrid city environments.

# 5 AN IMPROVISATION-BASED MODEL FOR URBAN INTERACTION DESIGN

Script and reality are incompatible.

—VITALY MANSKY, filmmaker

By identifying, throughout these past chapters, the interactions in and with urban responsive environments and the art of improvisation as fundamentally related topics of investigation, I propose to identify these four key positions that are recurrent in different types of improvisation and that together point toward a foundational model for urban interaction design: (1) open beginnings, (2) timing and agency, (3) understanding in action, and (4) unexpected interactions. These four positions provide a framework by which responsive systems and environments in the context of the hybrid city might be more systematically understood and developed.

## OPEN BEGINNINGS: DESIGN FOR INITIATIVE ENSURES OPENNESS

The best platforms allow room for user quirks, and they are open enough to gradually incorporate such quirks into the design of the platform. . . . Sometimes the best design is anti-design, which makes space for the accidental, the spontaneous, and even the bizarre.

—GEOFFREY PARKER, MARSHALL VAN ALSTYNE, AND SANGEET PAUL CHOUDARY, *Platform Revolution*

A man stands on the side of a busy road. No pedestrian crossing is near, and he observes the traffic, waiting for an opening, to step onto the road and make it safely to the other side. Other people stop near him with the same intent. They watch the cars go by; one of them half steps onto the road and then retreats as a speedy driver approaches with no sign of slowing down. Finally, a woman walks onto the road with determination, making the first step. Others follow. Now they are a group about to cross. Cars slow down, acknowledging this impromptu staging of a crossing. The group of pedestrians, without prior coordination, found itself cooperating. As they cross, they see a large mass of people walking around the corner farther down the street: protesters with signs held up high, people who have taken to the street unannounced, a flash mob demanding more control over what use is made of their personal information captured by social media platforms. The street, with its rules and regulations, its ordering lines and physical barriers, has become an open place for a new initiative.

A critical aspect of improvisational performance is its beginning and, as such, notions of agency and autonomy of a person or system. Who starts? When to start? How to start? As there is no plan, the beginning of an action is born out of context and out of initiative. Making a first move, speaking the first word, and taking initiative represent a marking of an unmarked space.[1] Improvisation is, however, not so much about creating or maintaining any one particular work but rather about ensuring an openness toward a process of ongoing creation.

I previously discussed Heidegger's description of the existential triangular relation between the artist, the artwork, and the art: while the artist makes the artwork, the artist is such only because of the existence of the work of art. And both the artist and the work of art exist only because of a prior recognition of notions of art itself—which, then again, exist because of the work of the artist and the work of art.[2] It is the continuous creative act that maintains this triangular relation in existence, not any one single artwork itself. It is keeping up the process of making that ensures that the triangular relation persists over time. Similarly, in improvisation, it is not any one construct that is the result of an improvisation that counts, but, rather, the aspiration is to keep the process of improvisation going.

Designing responsive systems in this sense, then, implies viewing any process of interaction as something that has already begun as well as something that will continue beyond any specific instance of interaction while fostering openings for initiative. Systems that espouse this notion need to be sufficiently open so that human initiative can generate significant variations that become foundational for the interaction process itself.

To *act* means to *begin,* and it is in the very nature of beginning that something is begun that was not there before, that comes as a surprise, and that could not be expected.[3] Today's availability of massive amounts of data incidental to everyday human activity and generated in systems of telecommunication, transportation, health care, and the like is used as an often undisputed basis for the planning and operation of urban systems. These data, however, are necessarily based on past observations, and predicted future events are based on statistical models and probabilities. Hannah Arendt's writings caution that "the new always happens against the overwhelming odds of statistical laws and their probability" and that "the unexpected can be expected from him [the human], that he is able to perform what is infinitely improbable."[4] It is extremely tempting to use the vast amounts of historical and real-time data available from today's digital urban systems for the design of urban interventions using data-driven models. These data sets and data streams describe the behavior of large numbers of people in considerable detail and over extensive temporal frames, and they are often readily available from existing infrastructure setups. The approach essentially assumes that what could be observed in a statistically significant sample in the past is likely to repeat itself in the future. And this approach has been working rather well for the planning disciplines so far. It has, in some way, been an effective work-around for what is, instead, more challenging to accomplish: to enable ad hoc responses at the instance when a quest or challenge appears—for example, to connect with your city's administration right when you spot an issue to be addressed or to see a bus turn into the bus stop right when you arrive.[5]

Embracing Arendt's profound reflection in today's hybrid city context, I suggest that the hybrid city, with its pervasive networks of connected devices and digital-physical interfaces, need not be limited to plan- and probability-based operations. Quite on the contrary, a value of hybrid city technologies lies in the ability to facilitate and support ad hoc behavior and interactions, an acting in response to the moment and to a given situation, an ability to shift emphasis from statistical *probability* to actual and unpredictable *possibility*.

The question, then, is how to design systems for such improvisation-based interactions. The focus needs to shift to leverage today's technological context to support people's acting in the moment—how to design in a way that embraces the unpredictability of human acting, and how to use technology systems in the hybrid city in a way that fosters taking initiative. We need to consider how to design for an openness that allows people to bring themselves into complete interactions through their participation. For this purpose, I suggest revisiting Umberto Eco's *Opera Aperta* [*The Open Work*] in the context of the hybrid city.[6]

*Opera Aperta*, written in 1962 and translated into English significantly later, in 1989, has widely influenced the domains of art and design since its publication. The text articulates a change in the point of view of art and its perception that culminated around the 1960s. For centuries, the author of a work of art was seen as the sole source to instill meaning into the work. A passive audience would then receive from the artwork what the author had bestowed on it. *Opera Aperta* describes the shift in mind-set toward what we would now call co-creation. It argues that the performance, reception, and interpretation of the artwork are all active parts in the constitution of the work itself. The artwork is not closed by the author but is essentially open for continuous acts of interpretation and completion when interpreted and performed and interacted with by an active audience. The following three notions in Eco's argument are of particular interest to the issue of openness and initiative for improvisation-based

## Design for Initiative Ensures Openness

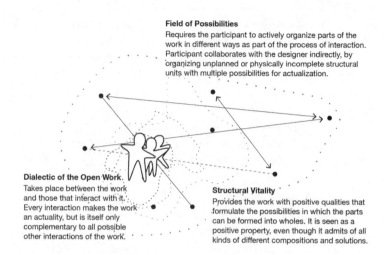

**Field of Possibilities**
Requires the participant to actively organize parts of the work in different ways as part of the process of interaction. Participant collaborates with the designer indirectly, by organizing unplanned or physically incomplete structural units with multiple possibilities for actualization.

**Dialectic of the Open Work.**
Takes place between the work and those that interact with it. Every interaction makes the work an actuality, but is itself only complementary to all possible other interactions of the work.

**Structural Vitality**
Provides the work with positive qualities that formulate the possibilities in which the parts can be formed into wholes. It is seen as a positive property, even though it admits of all kinds of different compositions and solutions.

Figure 1. Open beginnings: design for initiative ensures openness

interaction: (1) fields of possibilities, (2) dialectic in the performance of the open work, and (3) structural vitality of the open work.

### Fields of Possibilities

Open works are characterized by the intrinsic invitation to an active audience to make the work together with the author of the work. In an open work, the relation between the parts that make up the work is not entirely defined by the creator of the work; what the work is and how it behaves is deliberately under-specified by the creator.

Rather than as a composition, the Belgian composer Henri Pousseur describes his piece *Scambi* as a *field of possibilities*. The tape-music-based piece requires the listener to actively organize the parts in different ways before engaging in the listening part of the experience. The listener collaborates with the composer by organizing unplanned or physically incomplete structural units with multiple possibilities for realization; in this way, the listener is actualizing the composition at every instance while listening. By describing the work as a *field*, Pousseur moves beyond strictly causal relationships and a rigid, one-directional system in his work. Instead, he suggests a move toward a perspective of complex interactions between parts that every time newly reconfigures possible events into dynamic structures. The notion of *possibility*, then, discards a predetermined order given by the author and suggests a "devolution of intellectual authority to personal decision, choice, and social context."[7] In this way, *Scambi* always changes as it is organized and perceived by different listeners and at different instances.

Eco proposes his notion of the open work as a poetic theory, a theory of creation, and, essentially, a theory of design. This poetic theory puts into action and into tangible form systems that recognize *openness* as the fundamental possibility for both the creator and the consumer of the work. Constructing a *field of possibilities* in the context of the hybrid city, then, points toward creating interventions that do not play out in a way that is or can be controlled by the designer. Instead, the designer constructs *fields of possibilities* through an intervention in which audience engagement and different urban dynamics change the disposition of the field continuously.

Fields of possibilities relate to the notion of *lack* that Omar Khan identifies in his study of Canetti's crowd behaviors, Lacaton and Vassal's Palais de Tokyo with its expanded space of occupation left incomplete by the architects, and Tschumi's grid of follies at the Parc de la Villette.[8] Fields of possibilities are created by today's social running platforms (such as those operated by Garmin, Suunto, Fitbit), which allow us to connect with fellow runners via the routes they digitally generate by their practice and share with others through the platform. They enable virtualized and asynchronic competitions, mediated social interactions, actual meet-ups for shared practice, races, and similar events and activities. In this instance, the constellation of the connected mobile devices, the digital social platform, the participants, and the physical space are orchestrated to open up new potentialities. These are potentialities that become actualized anytime anew when participants "connect the dots" of this system. They are characterized by an openness that is continuously negotiated between human participants and the responsive elements as both condition and reflect each other's behavior.

This openness invites initiative and participation in the creation of what is unplanned and unforeseen. Fields of possibilities are not without constraints, however. Openness, for Eco, does not mean that anything is possible. Pousseur's *Scambi* could be rearranged, but the units were established by the author: the units were tapes, and the units were recordings of audio. The author of the open work, the architect or designer, oversees these kinds of positive characteristics when constructing fields of possibilities. Furthermore, the designer oversees *how* the parts can be connected and defines the *structural vitality* of the open work.

## Structural Vitality of the Open Work

Eco distinguishes an open work from any random collection of parts by elements of structural vitality. These elements make the open work susceptible to a range of integrations. "They provide it with organic complements which they graft into a structural vitality which the work already possesses, even if it is incomplete. This structural vitality is still seen as a positive property of the work, even though it admits of all kinds of different conclusions and solutions for it."[9] The structural vitality of an open work is composed of the positive qualities that formulate the possibilities in which the parts can be formed into wholes.

The open work offers a field of relationships within which possibilities arise. Such a field implies organizing rules that govern these relations. The author of the work, the designer or architect, offers this field of relations to an audience that through individuals' personal interpretation and performative engagement actualizes some of the possibilities of the work. The work offers such personal interventions, and the audience as an interpreter inserts itself into this field of possibilities. However—and this is key for Eco—the field of possibilities always remains the world intended by the author of the work. While the author does not know in which ways the work will be interpreted and actualized by an audience, that form remains tied to the author of the work—it is a form made possible through the original work that created the field of possibilities and its structural vitality. Mutability is a key factor in this dynamic. An open work is like a malleable material that can mutate into different forms, but every form is retraceable to that material. The mutability is deployed as a factor within limits authorized by the pliability of the material offered to the performer and audience for manipulation.

In the preceding example of social running platforms, the structural vitality is provided by the governance frameworks formulated by each platform, the ownership model, and the kind of currency (social or otherwise). For instance, as platform users run their routes, their GPS-equipped watches record and upload these to the platform. While this information is of value to each individual user, the accumulation of these routes informs other users' route choices in return at every iteration.

The intricate set of rules in David Brown's Available City, discussed in chapter 4, is the structural vitality that Brown *gifts* to his open work.[10] The rule is that developers can integrate up to five nonadjacent city-owned lots for their projects and that they can develop the lots for free as long as an area equal to the lot's footprint remains publicly accessible within the project developed on the lot. Whatever developments result from the Available City, they will be formed by these sets of relations established by the architect. However, none of these relational rules can predict any of the actual developments and the ways in which those developments become actualized as a result of the interplay among city, private developers, residents, and other stakeholders.

The structural vitality developed by the designer of hybrid city interventions becomes a generator. It is a catalyst for action and initiative, an invitation to take part in the completion of the project; this completion, however, is never fully complete but always only the beginning of a next act.

## Dialectic in the Performance of the Open Work

Adopting a perspective of a design intervention as an open work also means embracing a new kind of dialectic between the work and those who will perform it through their active participation. In every instance of performing the work or interacting with it, the work takes on a fresh perspective for itself. In Eco's words, "Every performance explains the composition but does not exhaust it. Every performance makes the work an actuality, but is itself only complementary to all possible other performances of the work."[11] In this sense, a work can generate endless meanings in the interaction with its participants. Every such interaction will unveil something about the nature of the work, but there will be more to it than can ever be uncovered. Furthermore, these different moments of interaction are connected, and so are the parts they uncover. Becoming aware of multiple interactions means expanding the awareness of the field of possibilities. Every actualization of the work, if aware of previous actualizations, contributes to a growth of the scope of the work. The work, so to say, *grows* on people and on people's habitat and place.

In the context of the hybrid city, this idea relates directly to recent developments of networked systems whose mode of operation is established continuously anew as the system is in actual operation. Only through the operation of the system itself do more permanent structures emerge that become meaningful. For example, the recently implemented dockless bike-sharing systems are generating concentrations of parked bikes as immaterial *emergent docks*.[12] Someone parks a bike next to one that was parked there by someone else. Another person chooses to park another bike right next to the two bikes, and so on. Throughout the territory of the shared bike program, such unscripted emergent docks form in different places and at different times of the day. They become part of people's understanding of how the system works. Nobody prescribes that mode of operation, and it could at any time change, adapting again to its context. It is a pragmatic kind of ethnomethodology in action, referring to Suchman's discussion, in that users of the service continuously learn about the ways through which the system is being constructed by the very acts of the users themselves.[13]

## Implications

A design approach focused on initiative and openness means to focus on interventions that are open to evolve over time, on the basis of what people make of them and how they appropriate them as part of their behavior.

In this view, a public utility such as street lighting, as an example, is not tied to being a fixed illumination in places where light poles are placed at the moment of installation but becomes an illumination of public space that can adapt and adjust in response to situations and behavior over time. The placing of the light sources and their orientation, intensity, and quality of emitted light need, in this perspective, to be designed in a way that allows for them to be changed dynamically. The modality in which these characteristics can and will change becomes part of the design process up front. And the way in which they can be changed needs to be intelligible and accountable, and this accountability becomes part of the design process as well. Designing improvisation-based public lighting, then, means designing the way in which light will *behave* in public space over time. It may even involve ways in which lighting structures will be positioned and repositioned in a time to come. Design, in this sense, is understood right from the beginning as a process of ongoing *redesign*.[14]

The design task at this point consists in conveying to people that they can bring themselves into this continuous process of redesign by conveying the openings, the changes that can be made—the *structural vitality*. This, then, becomes a *design for initiative*. It does not prescribe when and how to change something, but it constructs and lays out the *field of possibilities* within constructed systems.

In the context of today's hybrid city, there is a tendency toward automation of previously manual processes. However, a condition of openness and adaptation does not necessarily imply an automation of related processes. To remain with the example of public illumination, it is conceivable that sensor-based systems monitor pedestrian behavior and that the resulting data could be used to automatically condition specific parameters of public illumination in response and anticipation of human behavior. Alternatively, however, it is equally possible to construct a system that involves direct interaction by pedestrians in adjusting the direction of illumination, altering the quality of the emitted light, and similarly changing other characteristics. Opting for one or the other approach becomes a critical design decision that is part of a larger question about what kind of openness should be afforded through such a system. Even if the system is fully or partially manual in its operation, information technologies can contribute to this process by sensing behavior and interactions, and they can assist in system adjustments. The use of information technologies can reduce the latency of adaptive and responsive processes, shortening the time required for a response.

This idea leads us to the element of time in the context of improvisation and improvisation-based design. Responsiveness and improvisation can happen in a matter of seconds or less. We can consider them, however, also at a slower pace of several minutes, hours, or even weeks and months. The longer the temporal scale of responses to an action, the more critical the issue becomes as to whether a response is still understood indeed as a response to a specific event. And this leads us to the second position of the proposed design model.

## TIMING AND AGENCY: AWARENESS OF TIME ENSURES THE RELEVANCE OF ACTIONS

Everybody has a plan until they get punched in the mouth.

—MIKE TYSON

Consider the following situation: You walk along a street and see a friend coming your way on the other side of the road. Your eyes cross briefly, but both of you keep walking on. A moment later, you raise your hand for a friendly greeting, but as you carry out this salute, your friend has already turned away, walking on. Your gesture was not acknowledged as a greeting, and in the shared memory of the encounter, you did not actually greet your friend. The timing was *off*. The moment had moved on when you acted; the opening for a possible encounter had closed.

In improvisation, the temporal dimension is key. Improvisation happens in the present, and the presence is coproduced by performers and an active audience or responsive technologies in the context of the hybrid city. "It is no longer clear whether the presence is given to us or whether we, the spectators produce it in the first place," notes Lehmann in describing postdramatic theatre as *a performance that produces presence*. "Aesthetic time is not metaphorically translated historical time. The 'event' situated within aesthetic time does not refer to the events of real time."[15] Time, in the work of the Viewpoints improvisation technique, refers to tempo, duration, kinesthetic response, and repetition. The meaning of actions is formed by the configuration of content in both time and space. The improvised act is an act that collapses moments of planning and execution, and timing refers to the relationship between one moment of change and the next. The experience of time between such moments of change creates the openings for action, for choice. Through the choice to start, to stop, and to change, we determine our own experience.[16] Determining the timing becomes an expression of freedom to act.

Amazon's Wi-Fi-based *Dash* button in people's homes can be viewed as a machine that eliminates this time between moments of change. It is a machine that produces the elimination of choice. In contrast, a design approach with an awareness of time puts emphasis on the experience of time, the felt time or event time, rather than the chronological time of *chronos*. Hybrid city technologies need no time schedules; they adjust, adapt, and respond to change, to events, and to personal time. The kind of time that gains importance in an improvisation-based design for the hybrid city is a qualitative understanding of time, pointing to an idea of the right or opportune moment, when an opening appears for a committed action of opportunity.[17]

For an improvisation-based design informed by this position, we will look beyond clock time and at notions of *rhythm* and *kairos*.

## Awareness of Time Ensures the Relevance of Actions

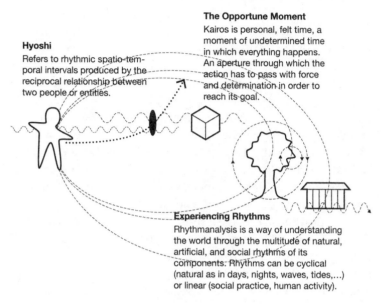

**The Opportune Moment**
Kairos is personal, felt time, a moment of undetermined time in which everything happens. An aperture through which the action has to pass with force and determination in order to reach its goal.

**Hyoshi**
Refers to rhythmic spatio-temporal intervals produced by the reciprocal relationship between two people or entities.

**Experiencing Rhythms**
Rhythmanalysis is a way of understanding the world through the multitude of natural, artificial, and social rhythms of its components. Rhythms can be cyclical (natural as in days, nights, waves, tides,...) or linear (social practice, human activity).

Figure 2. Timing and agency: awareness of time ensures the relevance of actions

## Hyoshi

In the Japanese martial art form karate, practitioners repeat the same sets of moves and techniques for years over and over again in their practice. This preparation, however, only seemingly leads to a planned and scripted behavior in a confrontation. In the years of practice of one single technique, every instance of the technique is unique and different every time, even if unapparent to the eyes of an untrained observer. During a confrontation, the sequence of actions is essentially improvised and a response to the unique situation at hand.

One of the ethical foundations of karate is to not strike first. Karate is essentially a defensive practice, but an attack can be considered part of a defense if the situation demands it. This, then, can seem a paradox: how to attack to defend without striking first.

One answer to the conundrum lies in the meaning of *sen no sen* and, as an extension, the Japanese concept of *hyoshi*.[18] *Sen no sen* consists in anticipating the opponent's attack *after* the latter has committed to the attack but not struck yet. Karate practitioners in their practice train for and achieve a heightened sense of awareness of the self and of their opponent. They pick up on actions that are about to be executed when they are still in their onset. Observation is focused on breathing, small levels of muscle contraction, and alterations in body posture. Awareness at this level enables a practitioner to capture the moment when an opponent has mentally committed to an attack, the moment when the opponent's body takes on the posture to launch an attack. A well-trained karate practitioner can recognize that moment and use this understanding to launch a counterattack that reaches the opponent before the opponent's attack makes contact.

It is possible to observe a similar dynamic in a prosaic everyday interaction. Think of a conversation between two or more people. One participant wants to speak up but is repeatedly anticipated (interrupted) by another person right when about to intervene. To do this, to anticipate such a speech action in its onset, we tend to observe movements in mouth, chest, and neck areas to pick up on signs of an inhale or muscle contraction before the utterance. We can call this a verbal form of *sen no sen*.

In karate also, the observation of the opponent includes the breath, the muscle tension, and, specifically, the triangular configuration between head and shoulders. Any body movement will begin with an alteration of this triangular configuration. Observing these cues allows for the timing of an action that changes the meaning of the situation. It can determine overcoming an attack by anticipating the action after it has been committed to and launching a defensive attack that follows the onset of an attack.

*Sen no sen* is part of an intricate understanding of timing, *hyoshi*, a key concept in Japanese culture more broadly. *Hyoshi* refers to rhythmic spatiotemporal intervals produced by the reciprocal relationship between two people or entities. It also refers to the *cadence* of each one of them, closely related to each one's breathing and mental state. Think of when you walk on the sidewalk and someone comes your way, right in the line of your path. Both of you walk straight toward each other. In such a situation, most of the time, you avoid each other by passing to the left or right. Sometimes, however, as you step to one side, the other person does so too; you step to the other side, and the other person does so again right at the same time. You continue to try to avoid each other's path but instead continue to block each other. The timing and rhythm of your movements is *off;* it is in discordance.

In a combat situation such as in karate, *hyoshi* describes the change of distance between two combatants as they move closer and farther from each other awaiting the opportune moment to launch their attack. There is a certain rhythm in those changes. Even when the combatants are not moving, there is rhythm. Muscles contract and relax, and there is breathing. There is a rhythm that is connected to movements that are being made and those that are about to be made. *Hyoshi,* in karate, has two aspects, one relating to oneself and one relating to the opponent. The practitioner enters into a rhythmic relationship with the opponent, finding one's own *hyoshi* by apprehending that of one's opponent. When the *hyoshi* of both is in close accord, the movements of the two complement and avoid each other. This can also happen without the opponents moving, remaining apparently still.

An opening for an attack arises when the *hyoshi* of two opponents is not aligned. Who takes initiative in that moment will find a vulnerability in the position and pace of the adversary. "Striking after having won," in karate, means purposefully creating a discord in the rhythmic harmony between oneself and the adversary. The opponent will still be adjusting to the change in cadence and will be off balance, not finding the *hyoshi* of the other. The strike then makes manifest the outcome of a confrontation that has already been decided at the level of *hyoshi*. At such high levels of practice, stories exist about confrontations in which no actual physical confrontation took place. The confrontation was won at the level of *hyoshi,* the level of timing and rhythm, and no actual strike was ever made.

*Hyoshi* is not limited to the martial arts; it is a concept with wider presence in Japanese culture. It is an integrated set of cadences that brings together as rhythmic elements several human subjects and their surroundings within the framework of an arranged activity. This integration of cadences results in a balance or an overall harmony. *Hyoshi* is present in the Japanese tea ceremony, also known as *chado, sado,* and *chanoyu.* The preparation and consumption of tea in the context of the tea ceremony take place inside a rigorously arranged space. It is performed by way of specific gestures that are blended with a mental state of harmony. The movements of individual participants take place in relation to each other and in relation to the physical environment and to the objects that are part of the ceremony. These movements happen in a shared time and place, which creates a series of interpersonal rhythms. The rhythm is established through working with objects and in relation to the entire environment. In Japanese culture, it is by entering into a relationship with objects that a cadence or rhythm is established. This rhythm allows us to enter into harmony with other human beings or with nature. In Japanese culture, objects are understood as connected to the rhythm of the gesture that is executed in relation to them. An object in this sense has *hyoshi,* has a rhythm that belongs to it and that it brings into an interaction. Each element of the tea ceremony, be it human or object, is regarded as an enabler that permits the harmony of the whole of the ceremony to emerge. *Hyoshi* is the rhythm of this union, the cadence for entering into this harmony with others.

### Experiencing Rhythms

The philosopher and sociologist Henri Lefebvre does not specifically mention *hyoshi,* but his work on "rhythmanalysis" seems profoundly inspired by it and shares a similar kind of sensitivity. In what is his last book, published posthumously, he acknowledges that "certain oriental practices come close to these procedures [of rhythmanalysis]."[19]

Lefebvre's work on everyday life had a big influence on thinkers and practitioners in France and Europe and, in particular, for the Situationist movement. Rhythmanalysis is part of this investigation of everyday life, though it is lesser known than his work on the social production of space.[20] The book on rhythmanalysis builds on Lefebvre's earlier work, in which he discusses space as a product of social practices, and it outlines rhythmanalysis as a method to analyze the rhythms of urban spaces and their impact on their inhabitants. Lefebvre's intention was to initiate a "new field of knowledge: the analysis of rhythms."[21]

Lefebvre suggests understanding the world through the multitude of natural and social rhythms of its components. For example, in observing a garden, we can observe the rhythm of a tree in its seasonal cycle on an annual basis. Then, there are multiple rhythms within a tree itself: a flower has its own rhythm of budding, growth, and withering, as does the fruit that follows; animals that live on or inside the tree have their own seasonal and daily rhythm. There are rhythms of human activity related to this garden: the change in ownership of the house of which the garden is a part over the decades and centuries; the changes that each owner has made while residing in the house; the tools used for the garden work and their own histories of invention; the routine maintenance required to keep these tools in working order; and so on are all examples of these rhythms. Rhythmanalysis is a way of understanding the world through rhythms—through the temporal behavior of all things natural, artificial, and social. Rhythms can be cyclical or linear. They are distinct but interfere with one another. "The cyclical originates in the cosmic, in nature: days, nights, seasons, the waves and tides of the sea, monthly cycles, etc. The linear would come rather from social practice, therefore from human activity: the monotony of actions and of movements, imposed structures."[22]

Nothing in this world, for Lefebvre, is inert. No thing as such endures unchanged. "The everyday establishes itself, creating hourly demands, systems of transport, in short, its repetitive organization. Things matter little; the thing is only a metaphor, divulged by discourse."[23]

Repetition and difference, a dichotomy discussed earlier in regard to the essence of improvisation, are also key to rhythm, as Lefebvre understands it. "No rhythm without repetition in time and in space, without reprises, without returns, in short without measure." There is a relation between repetition and difference, as "there is no identical absolute repetition, indefinitely. . . . There is always something new and unforeseen that introduces itself into the repetitive: difference."[24]

The rhythmanalyst is for Lefebvre someone who has a heightened awareness of these rhythms and is able to observe them. Rhythm is a mode of analysis to examine issues such as the urban. Lefebvre does just that as he describes his own observations from his window overlooking the plaza in front of the Pompidou Centre in Paris.

Tools and technologies shape some of the observable rhythms, and they can also help to detect and observe rhythms. Today's hybrid city is filled with technologies that facilitate a perception of rhythms that are otherwise not apparent to the human observer. Remote sensing networks enable us to "see" changing particle concentrations in the air, the movement of large parts of a city's population throughout the urban territory. We can "observe" a bus approach the bus stop before it is visible to the eye, allowing us to adjust our own rhythm to stroll to the bus stop and meet the bus upon arrival—a newly mediated kind of human-machine *hyoshi*. Real-time location-based information enables us to participate in events in an ad hoc manner without planning up front; participation in the moment through technologies of access invites us to the coproduction of presence.

### The Opportune Moment

We have discussed *hyoshi* as the rhythmic spatiotemporal intervals produced by a reciprocal relationship between two entities—a certain being in sync. In the context of *hyoshi,* an opening for action arises if a shift is introduced in the *hyoshi* between the two entities. *Hyoshi* depends on the ability to observe and become aware of one's own rhythm, one's own personal timing. *Hyoshi* is felt timing, and, in that, it is related to the notion of *kairos*.

*Kairos* is personal, felt time, as opposed to the quantitative *chronos* at the basis of clock time. *Kairos* was understood by the Greeks as a time lapse, a moment of undetermined time in which everything happens. Its nature depends on who uses the term, as it is a direct and personal experience of time. Its significance as the opportune moment traces back to the practice of archery, in which *kairos* refers to an opening, an opportunity. It is an aperture through which the archer's arrow has to pass, with force and determination, in order to penetrate and reach its goal. *Kairos's* significance as the right moment is also related to the practice of the weaver. *Kairos* is the critical time when the weaver must draw the yarn through a gap that opens for a moment in the cloth that is being woven. With these two related meanings, *kairos* is a fleeting instance in which an opening appears for forceful and determined action in order for the action to succeed.

Circumstances enabling such a success of an activity can change at any time, and *kairos* depends on the readiness to adapt to an always mutating situation. This improvisational readiness to use the moment leads to a conception of temporality that is nonlinear in nature. *Kairos* is time as a succession of discontinuous occasions rather than a duration or historical continuity.

*Kairos* was key to Greek rhetoric. It was at the basis of the ideal to speak opportune words at the right time to the right audience and in the right way. The relations between these factors change continuously. Rhetoric involves a listening to the moment and to the occasion and an acting in the moment, in accord with the rhythm of an environment.

In *kairos*, every moment is unprecedented and unique, and in reference to Lehmann, we could add that the moment holds a presence to be produced through the opportune act that relates with the place and with the audience. With time understood through *kairos*, there is a unique opportunity in every occasion, an opportunity to create meaning through a "will-to-invent," through the opportune act.[25]

## Implications

A hybrid city that turns to improvisation as a mode of interaction incorporates a temporality of *kairos:* event and felt time and a qualitative notion of personal time to which machine-based operations and interactions adapt. *Kairos* more than *chronos* is the time of the urban improvise. At this point in time, several urban services have done away with fixed time schedules, with using the clock as a machine to help with the coordination of activity within and across cities. We already improvise when we share our real-time location with a friend through our smartphones; we already improvise when we arrive in a foreign city and connect with like-minded communities through social platforms that mediate the encounter. *Kairos* is the time that underlies these rhythms of action and interaction. There is an opening now to conceive new artifacts and systems for the hybrid city that are based more deliberately on *kairos*.

Leveraging *sen no sen* in the context of the hybrid city points to strategies of anticipatory design that is not tied to data from the past but on real-time observations, offering opportunities for action and interaction, an opening to create meaning. *Sen no sen* for responsive urban environments means listening to the rhythm and *tuning in*. It means, in the simplest case, to slide doors and gates open in tune with the speed of the walkers' steps. It means slowing down the interactions for a person with a slower pace and catching up to the ambitions of a quick walker, typer, or touchscreen swiper. The speed of action in the hybrid city can give way to the rhythm of interaction, a rhythm that is negotiated every time anew in an encounter between human and nonhuman actors.

The *fluid~time* project by Michael Kieslinger was an early contribution to shifting the mode of operation of interactive urban systems from *chronos* to *kairos*, changing the way people arranged their daily activities on the basis of events, demand, and unexpected occurrences rather than fixed plans. The project was an early attempt to explore the full consequences of real-time information technologies in everyday urban life by coordinating human activity without plans or schedules but by ad hoc matchmaking of supply and demand, question and response.[26] Demand-responsive services that use dynamic information and dynamic services have since found stronger footing. Uber connects a car, a driver, and a passenger; Airbnb turns any bed, room, or house in cities around the globe into an opportunity for hospitality and local encounter; dockless bike-sharing services provide you wheels when you need or want them. These dynamic services come with strings attached; the rosy picture on the side of the user of these services is contrasted by violent impacts at other levels. Local home buyers face competition from investments in apartments to be rented via room-sharing platforms; existing transportation industries feel threatened by new forms of ad hoc, on-demand ride sharing. The conflict has only just started, and it remains to be seen how the dynamic equilibrium of cities will shift to accommodate these developments.

Meanwhile, many digital urban platforms face a challenge different from the quickness of real time; they face the challenge of identifying the end of a duration, the moment at which to end the broadcasting. While Yelp, Google, and Facebook have become platforms that are extremely able to spot new activities and broadcast them via their platforms, it is the end of these activities that is their challenge—how to know when a store has closed, when an event has ended, or, tragically, when a life has passed? User profiles live on in these platform environments, and meaning is lost at the long end of the time scale. Urban platforms capture the start of an action but are challenged to detect—and respect—the end.

## UNDERSTANDING IN ACTION: FORMS OF ACTION ARE UNDERSTOOD IN THE MAKING

When we perceive our environment, it is we who invent it.

—HEINZ VON FOERSTER, "On Constructing a Reality"

A girl and her friend untie the large blue-jeans-like fabric bag that is held together by a red drawstring. The bag opens into a blanket, revealing hundreds of Lego bricks of various shapes and colors. The bricks have been collected by the girl as well as by her mother since she was her daughter's age. New and old parts still connect, maintaining compatibility over generations. The two girls look at the parts in front of them, and without a plan and without speaking a word, they start to build. Block on block, the pieces connect into larger shapes. One looks at the other's construction, adding a part, changing others. At some point, they understand what it is that they are building. The girl looks for a specific part to build toward that idea. They discover parts on the fly and integrate them also; now the shape changes, and the structure becomes something else. Misunderstandings provide some of the most compelling ideas for what to build next. The girls' understanding of what it is that they are building evolves and is part of the process; it unfolds as they put the pieces together.

When performers work together in groups, their attention is simultaneously on themselves, their environment, and their fellow performers. In improvisation, every contribution becomes material to work with for others, and every act contributes to what came before. Action and response happen in the moment, and they become part of a collective creation of meaning that informs the interaction in real time. Cues are part of the action and can announce with or without intention what is about to happen. Cues are picked up and interpreted; they announce an act and are used to anticipate. Cues are not necessarily interpreted without error. Misunderstandings are contingencies of such interactions and become constructive new elements that are integrated in the action.

The *working with* the cues from another human or machine actor is also an expression of the fundamental "yes, and . . ." attitude that is at the basis of improvisation: whatever is contributed by any one performer is taken by others as valid material to work with. There is no stopping an improvisation on the basis of a contribution being considered inappropriate. No premeditated plan draws a definitive limit for inclusion. There is no discrimination of contributions on the basis of working toward a known form. Any form in improvisation is, instead, understood as emergent from within the interactions in practice.

Improvisational performers do not only understand form in the making on the basis of the coming together of elements in the moment. Instead, their actions include a heightened ability to consider forms in their future unfolding. A few notes are interpreted in the context of an expected musical phrase about to unfold; a first gesture can give away an entire sequence, and performers can work with that whole form that they recognize at the onset as part of their response. The meaning attributed to the form of the whole on the basis of a fragment of it becomes once again an original contribution to the collective interaction—an emergent form of *synecdoche,* if you will, in which the presentation of the part leads to a simultaneous construction of the whole in a dynamic of anticipation.

In this sense, this third position of the improvisation-based design model points to an ontology and epistemology that become essentially performative. Things are not so much what they are by themselves but rather what they become as part of a performance in a specific setting. This suggests a significant shift away from the cognitivist idea that *understanding precedes action* and toward a notion of *understanding in action.* "The individual will have to act so that he intentionally or unintentionally *expresses* himself, and the others will in turn have to be *impressed* in some way by him."[27]

In the design of urban interactions, this ability to recognize form in the making puts the focus on *cues* and *clues* and on the *indexicality of gesture and behavior.* As responsive environments detect and interpret human behavior, system adjustments made in response are interpreted at their onset by the very people who condition the change. In such a feedback loop, an important role falls to the system's accountability—the ways in which any responsive system or artifact is "observable and reportable" by a person who can, to some extent, make sense of an action in context so as to support interaction in a continuously changing environment.[28]

## Cues and Clues

Cues in interactions are signals for action. Accountability is key in improvisation-based interactions. It is key to understand to what extent actions are observable, what the cues are that can be observed. Picking up cues from humans or machines enables an anticipating of an action, enables an *inferring* from a mix of

## Forms of Action are
## Understood in the Moment

### Cues and Clues

In ensemble work, performers feed off and build on what others do, passing cues back and forth, consciously or unconsciously. Misunderstandings and errors happen; they are constructive noise that leads to the emergence of new structures.

### Accountability

This refers to how an activity or practice is "observable-and-reportable" in and by itself. It is not an added comment but an intrinsic and inseparable characteristic of the action.

### Situating Actions

They are actions taken in the context and in consideration of concrete and specific circumstances. The circumstances of our actions are continuously evolving and can therefore never be fully anticipated.

Figure 3. Understanding in action: forms of action are understood in the making

one's context-related understanding of the complete form of an action of which one only sees the onset. As Erving Goffman quotes the sociologist W. I. Thomas, "We do not as a matter of fact lead our lives, make our decisions, and reach our goals in everyday life either statistically or scientifically. We live by inference. I am, let us say, your guest. You do not know, you cannot determine scientifically, that I will not steal your money or your spoons. But inferentially I will not, and inferentially you have me as a guest."[29]

Cues from interactions are signals for an *etiquette* of a place; "when an individual appears before others his actions will influence the definition of the situation which they come to have." Others will necessarily respond to these actions, be it passively or actively, and through their response, they will "project a definition of the situation."[30]

In the context of screen-based interface design, the work with cues has a tradition. Icons bounce to inform users of applications that are starting up or require attention, and windows pop up with alerts. More recently, haptic cues provide notifications at the periphery of attention through the connected watch on the wrist or the smartphone in the pocket.[31]

Also, beyond the screen, there is a history of designed cues: the dimming of lights in theaters announces the start of the program, a yellow traffic light announces the imminent red light, and the flashing light at the supermarket checkout signals a request for help.

The cues provided in all of the foregoing cases are signals of actions that are about to happen or that are in the process of happening. They help humans to understand a machine-based action, or, even more, they enable humans to *anticipate* or *interrupt* such an action.

The interactive-media scholar Greg Corness and the media artist Thecla Schiphorst explore how the interaction between theater performers and an autonomous generative music system can use synthetic sounds of breath as a cue for an upcoming action to incorporate the performers' sense of intuition.[32] Breath is used as an expression of intention for action and behavior. Before performing an improvised musical phrase, the system emits a breath sound specifically formed by the structure of the musical phrase that is about to play. The musical improvisation itself is generated from the monitoring of performers' movements within their environment and is modeled on two components of Viewpoints improvisation: performer motion and architectural shapes (lines and shapes) as detected in the environment. The results that Corness and Schiphorst obtained from interviews with performers indicate that when the system improvised and "announced" the improvisation by its synthetic breath, the improvisation was perceived as more understandable, facilitating performers connecting with it.

The Mechanical Ottoman project, developed by the design and engineering researcher David Sirkin and his colleagues, explores behavior types of autonomous objects and people's reaction to them.[33] Specifically, the study describes an experimental setup in which a remote-controlled ottoman is moved in ways so as to prompt a person sitting in an armchair to interact with it, to put the feet on it, to take the feet off, and so on. While the study relies on a remote-controlled behavior in the experimental setting, it points toward an autonomous object that would improvise its behavior in response to context and behavioral cues from a person. In the initial experiment, in which the ottoman was controlled by a human, the object presented, indeed, an improvised behavior (even if enacted by a human through the object); the later study transferred the motion control entirely to the object by automating the ottoman, though scripting the behavior rather than enabling it to generate responsive patterns of behavior.

For a design approach that works with cues to support the anticipation of an action, it becomes important to define when a system commits to an action after the cue. This means designing the announcement of an imminent action and the modalities and openings for an interaction that can actually change the action that was about to happen. As a consequence, a person interacting with a responsive environment needs to be able to interrupt the system's action regardless of whether an imminent action is understood or misunderstood. In this way, an improvisation-based design approach focused on *recognizing forms of action in the making* represents an opportunity to contemplate new forms of what we could call a *design for interruption*.

### Accountability

When observing an improvisation as a spectator, it is mesmerizing to see the back-and-forth of cues between the performers as they co-create their performance. It is surprising to observe that while many cues are given, only some are responded to and taken up by others. Performers in the moment direct their attention and at times become aware of cues from others, and other times they do not. Performers also choose deliberately whether to engage with a cue. In either case, the act of improvisation builds on the observability of actions of others. In such a way, actions create openings for engagement.

The observability in improvisation relates to Harold Garfinkel's notion of *accountability*—the "observable-and-reportable." Accountability for Garfinkel implies a being "available to members as situated practices of looking-and-telling"; "such practices consist of an endless, ongoing, contingent accomplishment."[34] Paul Dourish, whose work focuses on the intersection of computer science and social science, in his close reading of Garfinkel, adds that "the accountable aspect of activity is never a 'commentary' on the activity, standing separately from it; rather, it is an intrinsic and inseparable feature of how the activity is woven into the fabric of action and interaction."[35]

The cues of performers in an improvisation are the performance; they are not separate signs that are external to what is being performed. Similarly, interactions in the hybrid city need to be observable and accountable in themselves and through the very process that is observed. "The analytic concept of accountability emphasizes that the organization of action, as it arises in situ, provides others with the means to understand what it is and how to respond in a mutually constructed sequence of action. It turns our attention away from simply the perceived result or outcome of an action, to include how that result is achieved."[36]

In improvisation, as the focus is on an ongoing process rather than any specific outcome, the accountability of actions is essential for any engagement between performers. Musicians watch each other's body posture, glances, and nods closely to capture the cues and clues that are part of music making, that reveal the intention of a player, and that create the opening for another musician to step in, to take over, or to play along.

## Situating Actions

Improvisation works when performers listen and engage with their environment and with the situation. As discussed earlier, in Lucy Suchman's account of the Trukese practice of navigation, the Micronesian seafarers are guided by an in-the-moment interaction with the situation at hand rather than following an a priori plan. Their action is contingent on the circumstances that the moment presents and that could not have been anticipated.

Suchman also gives the example of running a series of rapids in a canoe to illustrate the role of the plan in the context of situated action.[37] Before setting off into the water, one is well advised to closely observe the topography of the riverbed, its turns and rocks. One would also make a plan of what route to take, what parts to avoid, where to turn, and so on. During the action, however, the waterway and the canoe will interact in unexpected ways, and while the initial plan was a good tool to get started and to have some reference points, one would be a fool to insist on following any such plan as the canoe makes its way through the water in a way that is unique to every run. "The purpose of the plan in this case is not to get your canoe through the rapids, but orient you in such a way that you can obtain the best possible position from which to use those embodied skills on which, in the final analysis, your success depends."[38]

Looking back at one's course of action, it may appear as if one was following a premeditated action all along, but this may say more about our way of analysis than about the actual course of action in all its detail and interrelations. At times, the very goal of an action may only become apparent after a series of actions, and it then may seem as if that was intended to be achieved from the start.

### Implications

An example for a design intervention that leverages accountability in urban interactions is the move by the Boston public transport agency, MBTA, to change the real-time digital signage in subway stations from the one-message format, "train arriving," to three distinct messages: "train *approaching*," "train *arriving*," and "train *boarding*." These events were already present in the data of the train-control system; revealing them to the passengers turns them into observable cues that allow for an engagement: passengers can act more in sync with the trains. Furthermore, an acknowledgment of situated actions on the side of passengers was the addition of digital signage outside the stations in addition to those on the platforms. In this way, passengers can see the state of upcoming trains in or near the station before speeding up or down the stairs to get to the platform. The intervention slows down the *rhythm* between trains and passengers and opens up opportunities for more successful matches between the two.

To design systems that are accountable refers less to whether an account of the system's actions is given. Rather, the focus is on whether a system is, by its nature, capable of providing such an account. Consider as an example a system of shared digital screens that is installed in a public environment to be used flexibly by citizens. Accountability of the content broadcast on these public screens can be considered in multiple ways. One way would be to require a physical connection (e.g., a cable) between the screen and a broadcasting device (smartphone, laptop, or similar). The accountability of the broadcaster would in this way be ensured by having the broadcasting person in the same place and physically connected to the screen via his or her device. With a remote connection to the screens, instead, content accountability could be enabled via a registration system that requires a participant to log into the system using personal credentials. In either case, whether these strategies are actually used to account for the identity of the broadcaster in relation to the broadcast content is secondary when considering the essence of Garfinkel's notion of accountability. The key is whether the system is designed in a way that makes accountability intrinsically possible.

In making actions in the hybrid city "observable and reportable," visualizations of data generated by hybrid city systems have received significant attention recently. Visualizations have proven more effective in representing these masses of data rather than numbers and words. "Words and sentences must, by necessity, come only one at a time in linear, logical order. Systems happen all at once. . . . To discuss them properly, it is necessary somehow to use a language that shares some of the same properties as the phenomena under discussion. Pictures work for this language better than words, because you can see all the parts of a picture at once."[39]

As a conceptual metaphor, the macroscope has been invoked to describe tools that "help us understand complex systems" in the wider design field and in the context of data visualization specifically.[40] Joël de Rosnay, the inspiration for this metaphor, in his eponymous book, describes the macroscope as being a tool for the big picture, a tool that enables humans to see and understand the connections between the parts and the kinds of their relations: "Today we are confronted with another infinite: the infinitely complex. We are confounded by the number and variety of elements, of relationships, of interactions and combinations on which the functions of large systems depend. . . . Now a new tool is needed by all those who would try to understand and direct effectively their action in this world. . . . I shall call this instrument the macroscope (from macro, great, and skopein, to observe)."[41]

Data visualizations have become a form of such a macroscope for the hybrid city. They are a tool—similar in nature to the microscope or the telescope—that stands in between the human and the world. They are a tool that conditions the very way a human perceives the world and interprets it. They are a tool that mediates a human experience of the world. Improvisation builds on observability of actions that are situated, and, in the context of the hybrid city, there is an opportunity to conceive novel forms of macroscopes that mediate between the inhabitants of the hybrid city and their networked world.

### UNEXPECTED INTERACTIONS: INTERACTIONS THEMSELVES ARE OTHER THAN EXPECTED

Each time I street juggle I use improvisation. Now, improvisation is empowering because it welcomes the unknown. And, since what is impossible is always unknown, it allows me to believe I can cheat the impossible.

—PHILIPPE PETIT, "The Journey Across the High Wire,"
TED2012

A man is tired from running his errands along a busy street. He comes by a docking station of the local bike-sharing system, which has a few bikes secured solidly in the docks. The man hops onto one of the bikes, puts his feet onto the fixed dock structure, pulls out his phone, and enjoys the unexpected opportunity to rest his legs while reading today's news. The docked bikes have become an unexpected form of public seating. They have a fee to ride but are free to sit on when parked.

In its unplanned and in-the-moment nature, improvisation deals with the unexpected and the uncontrollable. It essentially and at a significant level deals with that which cannot be fully known and consequently with what is *other* from what we know. Improvisation is acting without prior agreement, an acting in the absence of a provision made beforehand. It does not see the work with the unknown as a defensive tactic but embraces the work with the unknown productively and as a strategy to allow for novelty to emerge from interactions between actors.

The established design development process dedicates an entire phase to interactions between humans and constructed systems that are *other than expected*: the "beta phase." The beta phase is a test phase that acknowledges that things other than planned may and will happen as part of the interactions between humans and a product, system, or service. Users of a new device will appropriate and integrate that device in their everyday practice in their very own way. They will be oblivious to some of its intended uses, rejecting some of them while discovering other uses and modifying the device beyond a designer's imagination.

Beta test phases typically come to an end. The product or service gets wrapped up, finalized, and closed after any final modifications and fixes, after insights gained from the beta phase are implemented. Adopting an improvisation-based perspective for the design in hybrid cities is akin to acknowledging that cities and their interactions are always in a beta phase. Urban issues are, in the terms of Horst Rittel and Melvin Webber, never solved but are continuously *re*solved anew, with an acknowledgment of the shifting balance of positive and negative impacts that any intervention will have on different groups of stakeholders.[42]

## Interactions Themselves
## are Other than Expected

**The Other and the Wild**
Improvisation deals with the unexpected and the uncontrollable. Our culture has taught us to label the autonomy and otherness of things and creatures around us as wild.

**The Other and the Idiot**
The idiot is originally not the stupid and dumb, but the private citizen, who, unlike the public citizen, does not participate in public life. The term indicates someone that does not comply with expectations and causes us to think about the complexities of participation and the messiness of actual encounters.

Figure 4.  Unexpected interactions: interactions themselves are other than expected

Otherness is an element that is deeply entangled with the very nature of the urban condition. The choice to move to live in a city is in significant ways an opting-in to encountering the *unknown* and the *other* and to moving beyond the parochial sphere of the nonurban. Folding the art and practice of improvisation into the way we look at the design of interactions in today's hybrid urban environments means allowing for this otherness. It means allowing for the unexpected and the unforeseeable, embracing this other in the way we shape and actualize our environment.

### The Other and the Wild

The other, in its lack of being fully knowable and escaping control, can be a challenge, even a threat. Our culture has taught us to label the autonomy and otherness of things and creatures around us as *wild*: *wild* animals that can actually harm, the *wild* and uncontrollable behavior of an upset child, *wild* mushrooms that are potentially poisonous, and so on. The term denotes an absence of control, of understanding, and it resonates with a level of risk and threat, whether real or perceived.

In "The Trouble with Wilderness," the environmental historian William Cronon contrasts *wildness* with *wilderness*.[43] Wildness encompasses the uncontrollable and potentially dangerous authentic nature untouched by humanity. The concept of wilderness, instead, emerges in the romantic period as an idealized concept of nature that is tamed and sublime. Wilderness is seemingly natural but curated and controlled by humanity, such as in the case of national parks and other forms of protected landscapes.

Does the hybrid city give room for outright authentic forms of wildness, or does it contain it and produce it in its tamer and controlled form as wilderness, which corresponds to a romantic idea of an "other" as familiar and similar to the known? It is a delicate undertaking to describe manifestations of wildness in the hybrid city. When the wild can be described in words, when it is given a name, it is understood and tamed. It becomes familiar and loses its wildness and fear, just as in Peter Handke's drama *Kaspar:* "Already you have a sentence with which you can make yourself noticeable. . . . You can explain to yourself how it goes with you. . . . You have a sentence with which you can bring order into every disorder."[44] Furthermore, things are wild to some people and not to others; the wild is relative to one's own ability to deal with difference, diversity, otherness, and fear.

Trying to tackle the delicate task of identifying wildness in the context of our argument, I suggest considering the following examples on a continuum between the poles of wildness and wilderness.

Consider the mobile and connected work culture of *work anywhere and anytime* that is manifest for today's knowledge workers in some parts of the globe, as they leave the traditional office and work flexibly in a park, at a café, or perhaps holding a conference call with colleagues in another part of the world in the middle of the night to accommodate time-zone differences. Is this the formerly ordered and controlled cubicle workplace turned wild, or is it rather a wilderness-like condition of a romantic idea of freedom to work at will? Could it also be, rather, a diffused sense of obligation of being always reachable, always connected to work?

The Occupy Wall Street movement may be an authentic instance of wildness. Its acts of collective dissent and protest are mutually enabled by continuously changing forms of appropriation and tactics of networked media technologies that connect at the local and global scales. The network of unpredictable actions forms what the architects Jonathan Massey and Brett Snyder describe as the *hypercity:* emergent fields of actions, untamable and threatening to established orders; freedom for some but a fear of loss for others.[45]

Consider the human traffickers who sell hope to Syrian and African refugees and migrants to reach a place of peace and better life at the cost of a deadly journey across the Mediterranean Sea aboard overfilled and unsafe boats. The purpose and intent are different, but the network of traffickers uses similar tactics and technologies as the Occupy movement. Equipped with cellphones, the traffickers use social media to attract their clients and establish and change boarding locations and times as well as routes on the basis of real-time information received from a network of informants to avoid interruption of their activity.[46] This is a booming business to some people, hope of freedom to others, and a threat to still others. The perceived threat to some has, in 2018, even arrived at instances of Europe closing its ports to ships carrying shipwrecked migrants on board.[47]

The otherness that Cronon attributes to wildness relates directly to the capital-*O* Otherness in Jacques Lacan: the provocative, perturbing, disturbing enigma of the Other as an unknowable (which is different from Lacan's lowercase-*o* other, used when referring to the other as an alter-ego, imagined as being like oneself). The questions that Cronon raises about our nostalgia for wilderness are profound. They point us to ask whether the Other must always bend to our will. Or, if not, under what circumstances should it be allowed to flourish without our intervention? What risks are we willing to take to also allow for the potentially harmful facets of the wild to unfold? The concept of wildness is one that follows its own rules, one that evolves in response to many diverse factors also other than human and that cannot be fully understood by humans.

## The Other and the Idiot

It is seemingly preposterous to advocate for the role of the *idiot* in the *smart* city given the latter's insistence on rational thought and efficiency. Jennifer Gabrys, however, does just that when engaging this conceptual figure in the context of participatory digital urbanism.[48] Leveraging the Belgian philosopher Isabelle Stengers's work, Gabrys discusses new practices and forms of understanding of citizenship that emerge within the smart city.[49] She critiques pressures toward efficiency, solutionist approaches, and problem solving in the smart city domain. As cities and citizens become functional data sets that are managed and manipulated, Gabrys argues for a new understanding of citizenship that involves notions of becoming and belonging. These new forms of participation and citizenship depend on the disruptive figure of the idiot.

Stengers builds on work by Gilles Deleuze and on the ancient Greek origin of the term *idiot*. There *idiot* was used to describe in a nonderogatory way the *common man*, the *private citizen*, who, unlike the *public citizen*, in the form of the professional, the public official, or the expert, does not participate in public life and does not contribute to the common cause. The term is not associated with dumbness or stupidity, nor is it understood as simply not following rules. Rather, it indicates someone who does not participate in the way that is expected of a public citizen.

In this perspective, the idiot is someone or something that causes us to think about and encounter the complexities of participation and social life as something *other* than prescribed or taken for granted. It is someone or something that does not satisfy and comply with expectations, someone who, in the face of efforts to eliminate unpredictability through statistical models and surveillance, becomes a reminder of the messiness of actual encounters and of the impossibility of total control.

Initiatives of participatory digital urbanism such as various forms of "fix-it" services (such as the U.S.-based 311 and SeeClick-Fix and the U.K.-based FixMyStreet) build on and take for granted a kind of participation from citizens that happens as planned. The citizen is expected to comply with the given tasks and respond to the questions asked on forms to be filled out. The idiot, instead, is the citizen who does not respond as expected, who does not conform to the prescribed format of participation. Instead, this conceptual figure responds to the specific situation in a *personal* way, not in the accepted and expected way of a public citizen but as a private citizen. The idiot responds to the request to report potholes by bringing up issues that are of a personal nature in a specific situation. By doing so, the idiot *slows things down*. It slows down the push for making processes efficient; it slows down the way in which citizens are expected to participate in efficient processes of fixing things in the smart city. It slows things down by bringing up unexpected issues that are *out of place*, that are foreign to the established goals because it has in fact not agreed to them.

The conceptual figure of the idiot casts doubt on the implicit expectation of a conforming audience and is a critique of the underemphasis of issues related to the emergent and relational character of a situation. It does not respond to and interact with the digital tools of the hybrid city as expected. The idiotic act is one that deviates from the norm, from the expectation, from what was intended to be the citizen's prescribed—scripted—behavior and instead brings in what matters personally to a specific situation.

By defying expectation, the idiot brings up issues—of a different kind of value—that had not been considered. It relates in important ways to improvisation, since in both cases, action happens outside the constraints of a provision or agreement. Both do not follow a plan or script but respond to the specific condition of a situation. Instead of conforming to the norm, they thrive in and are able to act within the context of uncertainty. In the sense that they do not correspond to expectation, both the idiot and the improvised act are valuable resources in the context of the hybrid city, as they necessarily engage in expanding the field to include what is beyond expectation but what is indeed possible.

## Implications

Designing to embrace Otherness includes but goes well beyond design approaches that accommodate notions of diversity. Design for Otherness means allowing for the unexpected to happen and to be taken constructively by the interaction afforded by a designed system. Aspects that become salient are *redundancy, tolerance, robustness,* and *resilience.* Planning redundancy in designed systems and objects allows for superfluous parts to take on meaning in the course of interaction, to be appropriated beyond any scripted function or behavior. Redundancy increases possibilities for unplanned interactions. It increases the possibility for diverse unforeseen connections and interactions.

The hybrid city allows for unprecedented levels of control, and if we acknowledge that the attractiveness of cities lies in large part in encountering the *Other,* rather than oneself and the known, a design focus on Otherness is an antidote for letting ourselves get carried away by the deceptive allure of total control. Control centers are an expression of the will to suppress Otherness. They are periscopes to keep an eye on things, periscopes that all too easily become a panopticon. Once a control center is established, it cannot help but detect and counteract forms of deviation. Its very reason to be is to detect things that are out of control and rein them in.

A design approach that embraces authentic Otherness points toward a design for more tolerance, for more ab-use, for more *idiotic* use, and for more *wildness* in hybrid cities. This may generate discomfort. And it might be that this is not a bad thing, that it is a turn toward *discomfort* that can help bring out the best of ourselves.

## WORKING WITH THE MODEL

The model for the design of responsive systems in hybrid cities defines four positions that provide a framework of relations for the analysis and for the synthesis, the creation and development, of urban interventions. The purpose of the model is to bring those aspects to the foreground that are of particular relevance to the new and emergent condition of the hybrid city.

A model is always an approximation, a simplification articulated in a limited number of key components that link it to what it represents. While the model is by definition an abstraction from the specific and peculiar in order to identify relations that relate to multiple instances, a model's limitations come to the surface in its application and use in practice. Any model proposed for the context of cities, however, is confronted with the diversity of cultural, economic, and political contexts in cities of various scales. The improvisation-based design model is characterized by a focus on openness, adaptation, and iteration. To meaningfully employ this model, the recursive back-and-forth that is inherent in improvisation and in the improvisation-based design model becomes part of its mode of operation and application. In a certain sense, the model ought to apply its own positions toward itself in its application. In this way, the openness and indeterminacy of the model becomes partial and tactical in nature, and it operates through adaptation to specific situations rather than being applied in a universal way.

# 6 EXPERIMENTATION WITH UNCERTAINTY AND THE UNPREDICTABLE

> When we reach the future, the actions thought up in the past are no longer relevant. While we were spending time thinking, our environment changed. Our context is different.
>
> —RUTH ZAPORAH, *Action Theater*

The value of a new design model lies in its utility to construct future interventions, making use of the positions identified by the model. Another value of such a model lies in critically reviewing existing projects and interventions through a new perspective for a new understanding.

This chapter employs the improvisation-based design model presented in chapter 5 to examine four existing projects. The projects display some of the characteristics of improvisational dynamics discussed so far. They represent instances along a trajectory toward an improvisational perspective on the design of urban interactions.

Not all of these examples display all elements of the model equally, but all of the examples display some of these elements to some extent. Examining these projects by way of the four positions of the improvisation-based design model helps illustrate how parts of the model can be used in a design process.

I selected the following projects to cover urban interventions on a range of scales with regard to their relations with the physical environment as well as with their socioeconomic context. These projects allow me to discuss the improvisation-based design model in relation to real-world projects and to tease out its potential.

## DOCKLESS BIKE SHARING

Today's latest generation of bike-sharing systems have done away with the docks, consisting in the bikes alone. Bikes can be locked whenever and wherever the user completes a trip. The bikes are physically scattered throughout the urban territory without any planning, and yet they remain connected to a remote sensing platform. This latest breed of dockless bike-sharing systems builds on a remarkable history of bike-sharing modalities that goes back half a century.

In 1965, the Dutch counterculture movement Provo proposed the White Bicycle Plan to solve Amsterdam's inner-city traffic problem. The plan was for the city of Amsterdam to purchase twenty thousand white bikes annually to be distributed unlocked throughout the city. They were to be considered public property and free for everyone to use at will. When the city of Amsterdam did not take up this plan, Provo went ahead alone, painted fifty bikes white, and distributed them around Amsterdam's inner city, unlocked and free for everyone to use.

The white bikes were soon taken out of circulation by citizens for private use, as well as by the police, who confiscated white bikes in circulation on the basis of legislation that requires bikes to be locked when parked in public spaces. The bikes were returned to the Provos, who, in a second attempt, installed number locks on all remaining bikes, painting the numeric code onto the bikes to bypass the legal impasse. The system did not live on for long, however, as bikes were frequently damaged and stolen, and the White Bicycle Plan soon came to an end.[1]

The first large-scale bike-sharing systems were installed in 1995 in Copenhagen (the ByCyklen project) and in 2001 in Vienna (the Gratisstadtrad project first, followed by the Viennabike project in 2002). Both systems used dock stations, painted bikes, advertisement on the bikes to finance operation, and a coin-based docking mechanism similar to some supermarket shopping carts still in use today. A coin was used to unlock the bike at the dock, and when locking the bike at another docking station, a coin of equal value was retrieved.

Vélib in Paris launched the third generation of bike-sharing system in 2007, operated as a concession by the advertising and street furniture company JCDecaux. The innovation that set this third generation of bike-sharing systems apart was the requirement of a personal identification and a higher deposit for the use of the bikes. In order to register with the system and unlock the bikes, the use of a credit card or a cellphone number was required. Holding a larger deposit through the credit card and requiring personal identification helped these systems avoid vandalism and theft of the bikes.

Today's dock-based bike-sharing systems operate essentially in the same way as the Vélib system. The main components are docking stations with wired or wireless telecommunication, a kiosk interface to use with a bank card for registration with the system, and bikes that contain a docking mechanism that is mechanical and contains a digital connection to identify the specific bike connected at each dock.

A key issue for the operation of these systems is the so-called balancing of bikes between the dock stations throughout the day. Trucks move bikes from stations with excess numbers of bikes to other docks with too few bikes. The purpose of this is to balance the system and counteract dynamics by which many people use the bikes to ride from outer districts to inner-city locations in the morning and then the other direction during the evening commute. The precise strategy for rebalancing is complex and also considers predicted demand patterns based on the analysis of historical data.

The latest generation of bike-sharing systems from the past couple of years has introduced a significant innovation to the bike-share operation. It brings bike sharing surprisingly close to the operational practice of the first system of White Bikes in Amsterdam. This new generation of bike-share system does away with the use of docking stations throughout the city; the system is *dockless*. The first dockless bike-sharing operator, ofo, launched in 2015 in Beijing after the founding of the company in the previous year by members of the cycling club of Peking University. The company has since expanded to numerous cities internationally.[2] Also, competing dockless systems have entered the scene, such as the companies oBike, LimeBike, and Reddy.

These dockless bike-sharing systems, as the name implies, operate without the need of physical docks to retrieve and return the bikes, as is the case of dock-based systems. The dockless system consists only in the bikes themselves. Bikes are parked anywhere in the city, and trips can start and end at any location. Unlike Amsterdam's early White Bikes from 1965, however, the bikes are now tracked by a sophisticated use of multiple systems. The bike location is tracked by a GPS system, and the lock mechanism is activated through the operator's smartphone app. In use, pointing the smartphone's camera at the bike lock's graphic QR code is sufficient to unlock the bike and pedal away. In order to conclude the ride, parking the bike in any public location and locking the mechanical lock is all that is required. Finally, using the operator's online map in the smartphone app helps to locate parked available bikes that are not in direct sight from a user's location.

The way these kinds of systems work technically varies slightly from system to system and from town to town. Some bike locks contain built-in GPS and cellular units. These systems always know the location of all bikes at any moment, during a ride and when parked. Other systems only have a Bluetooth connection in the bike lock and make clever use of the user's smartphone to get GPS location and cellular data transmission via the smartphone's Bluetooth connection. In this case, the system only receives the location during the locking and unlocking of the bike.

Where to park the bike is entirely up to the users in these systems, and this clearly provides room for interpretation and conflict. Several operators, such as oBike and LimeBike, give credit points to users for returning bikes to designated bike-parking locations. The credit system deducts points for parking the bike in illegitimate locations and for not locking the bike. Credit is also given for reporting bikes that are illegally parked or broken bikes.[3]

Figure 5. Dockless bike sharing. The latest generation of bike-sharing systems does away with docks entirely and works with GPS and Bluetooth technology, as well as QR codes in conjunction with users' cellphones. Bikes can be parked anywhere in the city, and trips can start and end at any location chosen by the users.

### Open Beginnings: Design for Initiative Ensures Openness

The dockless bike-sharing system appears to be characterized by a high degree of openness and invites users to take initiative. During everyday operation, and once you are registered with the system, whenever you see a yellow bike (in the case of ofo bikes) parked, you can walk up to it, unlock it, and pedal away at will.

The system reduces the cognitive and operational overhead. Riding a bike comes close to the immediacy of Amsterdam's White Bikes. When you see a bike in plain sight or virtually on a digital map, you walk up to it, unlock it with your smartphone, and start riding it, to then leave it parked at any spot. It is a strength of the system that it is so inviting and easily accessible; people come up with new ways of integrating these bikes into their daily routines that they themselves did not consider before.

The openness of the dockless bike-sharing system lies in that it offers enormous room for interpretation of how to appropriate and integrate the service within one's everyday routine: ad hoc acceleration of trips that add the convenience of a bike to what was planned to be a walk or public transport trip or the use of a bike alone or together with friends for a bike tour of an entire day, without the need to return to any specific location, are just some of many possibilities. While writing this book, I saw a little boy ride his own bike, accompanied by his parents both on yellow ofo bikes. A family bike ride was made significantly more accessible because of the availability of these bikes. The bikes are painted in bright colors so that they stand out visually. Everybody who rides such a bike becomes an apparent model for others to see with regard to what can be done with the bikes, where they can be parked, and where they can be found.

The *structural vitality* of the project comes from the effective orchestration of functionalities from networked technologies and system governance. The GPS of the user's smartphone locates the bike during the unlock operation, and the phone also provides connectivity to communicate the bike's location and the user's identification to the bike operator's system. The QR code, scanned by the phone's camera, has finally found a worthwhile use, after having been around for years in search of a meaningful application. Implemented in this way, the QR-based bike-unlock mechanism turns a limit of the QR code into a feature: the requirement of a direct line of sight to visually scan the code ensures that whoever unlocks the bike is physically present at the location of the bike; a remote unlocking by users becomes impossible due to the deliberate use of the constraints of a technology.

The *fields of possibility* in this bike-share system are quite strikingly circumscribed by the omission of elements. Taking the docks out of the equation, the field of possibility is continuously re-created by the users of the system and their choices of where they park the bikes. This is a significant change to pay close attention to: the users of the system cause a continuous redesign of the system itself. This is not a system based on balancing average ridership demand, as is done in the case of dock-based systems.

Here, every single decision of where to park a bike matters, and each decision impacts the system significantly with regard to what possibilities are offered. A bike might just be parked literally outside your door one day and offer you a ride.

There are limitations to the openness of the system, however. Dockless bike-sharing systems largely require the possession of a smartphone as well as a credit card for payment. Some exceptions exist. LimeBike in Seattle, for example, introduced cash payments in 2017. People can prepay in cash at a physical office in the city and then call a number from any phone to have a bike unlocked.

These systems also tend to be limited to municipal boundaries; they rely on agreements with municipalities. In 2018, thousands of dockless bikes were being deployed in towns around Boston. "Notably absent from that list [of towns] are Boston, Brookline, Cambridge, and Somerville—the four communities that use the Hubway system. Their agreement with the private company that operates Hubway bars other bike-share systems," comments the *Boston Globe*.[4] This is an interesting new territorial condition that is created by commercial agreements and that is defeated by the very nature of bikes being mobile enough to cross municipal boundaries anytime.

Rebalancing the system becomes even more of a challenge with dockless bikes than with their dock-based equivalents, as the individual bikes are spread out and often hard to locate. The system does get unbalanced, with bikes being rare near subway stations during the evening commute, as users are keen to use them for the last mile of their commute. Rebalancing strategies, however, do exist and are either truck based or user based via dynamic pricing/crediting schemes.[5]

### Timing and Agency: Awareness of Time Ensures the Relevance of Actions

The quickness of the unlocking operation in bike-sharing systems matters. Dockless systems are very quick. You point your phone's camera at the lock's QR code, and in only a couple of seconds the lock opens. The immediacy is essentially at the level of Amsterdam's White Bikes from 1965—we have come full circle. There is no looking for the nearest bike dock, no payment or other phone interaction needed, and no kiosk interaction. The quickness of the interaction and the physicality of it matters in this service. The system uses sophisticated digital networks, but it also uses the physicality of the bike and its lock as an effective interface.

There is no need for a user to decide up front on the destination of the trip. There is no need to identify dock locations at the end of the ride and whether dock spots are available to park the bike once arrived. The timing of the system is based on *kairos*, the opportune moment. You see a bike and decide there and then to use it. There is nothing else to consider to make this work operationally; it is an effective low-stakes commitment.

Rhythms, ever changing locations of the bikes, emerge where bikes can be found at different times of the day. As a user of the system, one becomes acutely aware of the rhythms of fellow bikers using the system and the flow of bikes from one part of the city to another and back again.

When parking the bike, a user becomes aware that the place the bike is parked will condition the next use of the bike: whether it will be found easily and whether it is parked at a place with much foot traffic. It is an element of *anticipatory design* that invests and involves the user *directly*. Essentially, as a user, you design the future findability of the bike and the point of access to the system on every ride.

### Understanding in Action: Forms of Action Are Understood in the Making

The dockless bike-sharing system is in constant flux. Bikes are parked in different locations all the time, and the system, in this way, is capable of adapting to changing conditions of traffic, housing, residency, and so on. Precisely because there are no predetermined docking stations, the parked bike locations remain relevant in the context of constantly changing urban conditions, as the locations are an expression of actual use.

Cues about the state and the behavior of the system are provided directly by the visibility of the bikes in the urban environment. Bikes are very visible, as in the case of the bright-yellow ofo bikes. It is easy to spot them when they are nearby, and it is easy to spot accumulations of several bikes at specific locations at certain times (such as subway stations, schools, and office buildings). It is easy to observe also that at these same locations, there can be no bikes at all at other times.

The system is understood by the physical and visual presence of the bikes in urban space when parked as well as when ridden. You become aware of these bikes visually when they ride by you. You see these bikes when they are parked on the sidewalk or at other public spots. You use the system when you ride the bike, and you observe the system when others do so. When observing the system, you are also using it, as you learn from observing the ever changing locations and concentrations of the bikes in your immediate environment.

Parking dockless bikes is fundamentally different from parking dock-based bikes. Where to park becomes an open question for the biker. There are indications of where to park: rules from the operator that urge users not to block the pedestrian way of passage. In the real context of sidewalks, finding an adequate spot to park leads users to become aware of the intricacies of public use of any particular spot. Parking these bikes is an excellent example of situated action, as you find yourself negotiating the affordances of tight sidewalks, lamp posts, and other elements to park the bike, abiding by the operator's rules as well as negotiating the contingencies of the actual characteristics of place.

Accountability beyond the bikes in plain sight is provided through the tracking system and the online maps. The bikes are GPS located, and wherever they are parked, they can be located. The trips of the bikes are also linked to the identity of the user, and thus there is accountability for potential damage to the bike, parking in spots deemed inappropriate by the operator, and similar criteria.

Unexpected Interactions: Interactions Themselves
Are Other than Expected

Today's dockless bike-sharing systems are *wild* systems. They are similar to Amsterdam's White Bikes. It is clear that anything can happen to these bikes, and a lot already has happened to them, from being "parked" on top of trees to being recovered from rail tracks and rivers.[6]

Bikes that do not have a built-in GPS unit can be transported to a different location while locked, and in this way, they can get *off the grid* quite literally. Their actual location no longer corresponds to the virtual one that is maintained in the operator's system and that is visualized on the digital maps of the system.

Cases exist in which bikes have been hidden behind dumpsters and bushes to "reserve" them for personal use at a later point, with users exploiting leeway in the system. Bikes are also frequently driven beyond municipal boundaries and dropped off in neighboring cities that have exclusive contracts with competing bike-share providers. This triggers operators having to recover bikes directly.

These uses are *idiotic*, as described by Stengers and Deleuze, in that they are acts by citizens that do not play by the publicly accepted rules.[7] They do not contribute to the common cause of the system in the way that the citizen is expected to contribute but instead represent personal interpretations of the system. They "slow things down." They are, however, by being *idiotic*, also a valuable manifestation of what is *possible*.

The otherness of the system is that you never know where to find a bike in advance. You can never be certain to find a bike nearby. That is different from dock-based systems, which are more predictable due to their limited number of bike locations, which concentrates bike availability, and across which operators balance availability. In a very concrete way, you cannot count on dockless bike-sharing systems, and yet they appear to work and fulfill a role. The balancing of the system does not refer to docks but literally to the entire urban territory. Some days a bike is outside your door; then again, on other days, the nearest bike is a several minutes' walk away. It is a system that does not allow you to settle in a "usual" mode of operation; it keeps surprising you, keeps you on your toes. The operation of dockless bike-sharing systems is fundamentally based on otherness. The system is always other than expected. It is a system that, in its current form, exists beyond control.

## PARKLETS

Parklets are extensions to urban sidewalks and cover what were previously parking lanes. They typically occupy one or more parking spots, consist in a base to make them level with the sidewalk, and have different kinds of furniture installed for seating, tables, planters, bike stands, and the like. The purpose of parklets is to provide for people space that was previously occupied by cars. Parklets are funded and installed by businesses such as cafés, bookstores, and restaurants to offer seating for their clients, but parklets are mandated to be open to the public at all times. They are seen to make the urban streetscape more attractive for walkers and turn a dull street into a destination. While seemingly permanent, parklets are installed in an ad hoc way that ensures easy and quick removal if needed.

The history of parklets really began in 2005, with a guerrilla-style installation by what would later become the Rebar Design Group. Driven by the desire to make sidewalks more attractive, group members occupied a metered parking spot with rolled-out grass, a planter, and a bench while feeding the parking meter. Since then, the third Friday of September has become Park(ing) Day in many cities around the globe as an annual event.[8]

Rebar received significant positive feedback about its friendly parking takeover, and the story did not end there. In 2008, the city of San Francisco reached out to Rebar to help initiate what became the first parklet prototype, a more permanent installation on parking spots sponsored by local businesses. The first parklet, the Divisadero Parklet outside the Mojo Bike Café, was installed in San Francisco in October 2010 after initial work on parklets was done in 2009.[9] Park(ing) Day inspired what has now become

San Francisco's Pavement to Parks program, which also coordinates the parklet initiative. The parklets are to some extent the experimental component of this more comprehensive program.

San Francisco's Pavement to Parks program has since developed a clear and accelerated process for the proposal, planning, and installation of parklets.[10] The initiative for a new installation comes from a business owner. The business puts together a first proposal and reaches out to the adjacent community to get feedback on its planned intervention. This feedback may lead to changes, and documented community feedback and support are required for the subsequent approval process with the city of San Francisco's public agencies. Community involvement is key in the process and has several functions: to get locals to accept and support the initiative and to tap informal knowledge in the local community to tweak interventions so that they will actually work. The outreach process by the business becomes a way of establishing the business itself as a "good neighbor" in the community. While the process has an ad hoc nature, the city has, by now, put in place a rather streamlined set of regulations that help guide the design and installation of new parklets. Parklets have become a testing sandbox for the city to explore new interventions that help make the city more attractive for pedestrians and promote a walking culture. The parklets seem to be a lose-win-win situation. While there is a loss of parking spots, community and pedestrians win in regard to an increase in attractiveness of sidewalks, and businesses win by establishing themselves in the neighborhood and attracting more business, as initial studies indicate.[11] The parklets initiative in San Francisco continues to be seen as a success, and it has since been adopted by other cities in the United States and abroad.

### Open Beginnings: Design for Initiative Ensures Openness

Parking spots are quintessentially scripted spaces. They are there for only one activity, to park one's car. They are governed by rules that dictate times of access and duration as well as the cost of parking.

Figure 6. Parklets in San Francisco: sidewalk extensions that provide space for people, covering one or more former parking spots. The installations are sponsored and installed by local businesses, developed in collaboration with the neighborhood community, and go through an accelerated permitting process with the municipality. A declared goal is to promote a pedestrian culture that leverages local initiative. (Clockwise from upper left: Swissnex Parklet, photo by Stella Kim; Exploratorium "Ciencia Publica" Parklet, photo by Stella Kim; Museum of Craft and Design Parklet, photo by David Leong, San Francisco Planning Department; 22nd Street Parklet, project and photo by REBAR Group)

The operation that parklets are involved in is a radical conversion from scripted urban space. The conversion is not prescribed; it rather opens up a space for conversation about what should become of that space. Parklets are a model case for participatory urban transformation, because the conversion process happens over a short period of time and because they concern an extremely small space that is visible and visitable by everyone. The first parklet installed in an ad hoc way in 2005 led, by the founders' account, to two people sitting down on the bench and planter and starting a conversation. An initiative gave way to another beginning of an encounter.

The program gives agency to local business owners and provides a way for them to engage with the local community to understand what it is that they desire to create in a plot of public space.

The parklet project is also opening up a contest for creativity among parklets. It is an open work because it really becomes completed every time people use it and appropriate it in their own way, as it is not limited to business clients but is mandated to remain open and accessible to the general public.

The *field of possibilities* of the parklet initiative consists in offering to *descript* a public space and open it up for participated improvisation. The field consists in this form of tabula rasa. It further consists of the participating actors and their needs, interests, and aspirations. The *structural vitality* of the initiative is provided by the mandated set of regulations and governance that describe the process of outreach and conversation beyond the constraints of construction.

Once built, every parklet expands the field of possibilities with regard to *what is possible* in a parking spot. Every new parklet and every use of all parklets recasts the field of possibilities of the parklet initiative, turning it into an ongoing act of participated and improvised place-making for cities.

### Timing and Agency: Awareness of Time Ensures the Relevance of Actions

Parking spots are spaces of time-based value and relevance. They serve a purpose when they are available, visible, accessible, and in demand by a car in search of one. As a consequence, the real value with regard to demand for parking spots changes over time. It changes throughout the day, and it changes over days of the week, over months, and over years as a neighborhood evolves.

The parklets still maintain some of the essence of this time-sensitive nature of the parking spot. The realization that a parking spot is a subsidized plot of real estate was at the basis of the first parklet installation in 2005. For only a few coins, the space could be rented. An additional realization was that things other than parking cars could happen on that spot.

The initiative to move to install a parklet outside one's business is an act based on *kairos;* it is an act that can happen in an opportune moment. Given that so many actors are involved in the establishment of a parklet and are required to support the initiative, planning and promoting a parklet becomes an exercise in awareness of *when the time is right*. It is out of this essential nature of the act that a deeper relationship of the business and the neighborhood community stems; the business did what was right for the place in the right time.

Park(ing) Day concentrates the temporal dimension further. Anything can happen as long as it happens within the twenty-four hours of the day. Park(ing) Day builds on the modularity of the parking spot and its clear markings as productive constraints. The requirement of quick installation and removal of the installation furthers the immediacy of the Park(ing) Day act.

## Understanding in Action: Forms of Action Are Understood in the Making

The formulation of a parklet is an improvisation over a prolonged period of time. Multiple actors take action, respond to proposals, and provide feedback. The improvised piece is the parklet. It has no real start, as the initiative by a business to start the path toward a parklet is always set within an existing dynamic between the business, the place, and its community. Actors involve the business, community members, the city's public agency, and architects and designers. The parklet evolves through the interaction of these actors and is based on the plan and the project document, which continuously evolves. The plan becomes not a prescriptive document but a document of work and of collaboration that informs and is informed by all participants throughout the process.

Parklets are site-specific manifestations. They are characterized by their uniqueness in structure and design, as they are formed by the concrete characteristics of the place and its socioeconomic interactions.

Parklets are an improvisation, as they are never complete but become completed anew with every use made and every modification enacted. A parklet's business promoter spends every day right next to the parklet and sees the use that people make of it. They witness the tension between use that was expected and new uses that passersby negotiate. If bikes are stacked on the side of the parklet, a modification to accommodate them better can swiftly be installed.

Parklets are an evolving manifestation of an improvised use of urban space; once installed, they take on the role of the plan in becoming the account of a continuous interaction between the actors who are interested and involved.

## Unexpected Interactions: Interactions Themselves Are Other than Expected

Park(ing) Day began as a subversive undertaking, an unwarranted claiming of car space for pedestrians. While the first parking spot installation by Rebar in 2005 was paid for by feeding the meter, the cordoning off and installation of grass, planter, and bench sidestepped existing norms. The group showed that, with little effort and time, a common type of urban space occupied by unused—parked—cars, and often not used at all, could contribute visibly to the quality of a pedestrian's experience of the city.

Rebar, in fact, observed in its first installation how two people sat down and began a conversation on its parklet. A parking spot had clearly been transformed to something other than what it was before. Park(ing) Day carries this idea forward. *Anything* can happen on a parking spot on Park(ing) Day. Things that happen there are experiments, twenty-four-hour model cases. In fact, parklets developed out of these temporary installations, which proposed an Other for what a parking spot could be.

Once installed, parklets develop a life of their own. While parklets are financed and installed by a business, access to them is mandated to be public at all times. Parklets have become an experimental ground for the city of San Francisco to explore what *other* can be done with urban space. Because of the connected nature of many kinds of activities, such as remote socializing, working, or gaming, these activities have filtered into the parklets. Parklets are not only the outdoor seating for a café; they become a temporary workplace for some people, a site for networked mobile games for others, and a place to rest, linger, and socialize for still others.

## WARDE

Warde is a responsive public shading and light structure designed by HQ Architects and installed in Vallero Square, in the heart of Jerusalem.[12] The project consists of four nine-meter-high and nine-meter-wide inflatable, flower-like structures. Each structure consists of a solid metal stem that has a large, inflatable red fabric mounted at its top hanging loosely from the stem when not inflated. Each structure is further equipped with an integrated air compressor, lights, and sensors. The structures are arranged in pairs at two locations of the square, which is divided by a tram line. The flower structures function as spectacular shading and lighting structures in a public setting and are visible from all around the square and from the nearby market.

The air compressor in each flower structure inflates the red fabric in response to context-related conditions such as pedestrian movement and arrival of trams at the station in the square. Wind further animates the fabric structures, and the sun position and sky condition determine the location and intensity of shading. Pedestrian movement is monitored by a set of cameras mounted at the top of the structure. Pictures are taken continuously of the area beneath and around each structure, and real-time image analysis provides data on pedestrian numbers, movement, and direction to be used as data input for the algorithm that controls the air compressor to inflate the flower structure. In addition, data from the public transport tram system are used to detect approaching trams, a factor that is also used for the behavior of the flower structures.

The behavior of the Warde structures is thus determined by a combination of several factors. For example, when pedestrians walk by one flower, it inflates and opens up. It then deflates and closes as people walk away. When the tram is approaching the station located at the center of the square, all of the flowers inflate together as a signal for prospective passengers. During a prolonged absence of any detected activity, Warde structures animate themselves using any random combination of some fifty patterns composed of different on/off sequences of the compressor. The fabric structures are constructed like surfing kites, and after being inflated, they deflate slowly, depending also on climatic conditions. An anemometer is mounted nearby to monitor wind speed.

The result is a group of structures that change shape as part of a complex set of interrelations among elements of their environment. Given the number of people typically present around the structures, the coming and going of the trams, and changing wind and sun conditions, the resulting behavior of Warde is highly complex. "Warde's attempt was not to fight the chaos [of the square], but instead to try and *tie the urban space together*, to spread around such fantastic elements that would overcome the reality of the square."[13]

## Open Beginnings: Design for Initiative Ensures Openness

Warde is a project that is completed every time anew when it interacts with its environment, which conditions its form. The project consists in a trunk-like rigid steel structure from which large petal-like inflatable sacks of red fabric are mounted. It is the surrounding environment that animates these petals. As a day at the square goes by, the movement of people, the coming and going of the trams, and the wind and the sun constantly change the form of the large flower-like shading structures.

The *field of possibilities* that the architects construct is defined by the definition of Warde's *sensitivities*—by defining, as part of the design process, of what changes in its proximity it takes note and to what kind of change it is sensitive. Defining this set of sensitivities, in the case of Warde, means defining the project's field of possibilities. The field of possibilities goes beyond the project's structures as such, however. It includes the spaces under

Figure 7. Warde, a large, flower-like shading and lighting structure in Vallero Square, Jerusalem, that interactively responds to activities in the square by changing its shape. (Project by HQ Architects, photos by Dor Kedmi)

and around that are impacted by their presence. The project's openness to its environment is as much determined by its behavior as by the specific two locations of the flowers inside the square and the constructed relation to pedestrian movements and those of the trams. Warde is a set of large and very apparent structures in a public square. When they change form, the appearance of the public square, as a whole, changes as well.

Warde is an open work, in that it requires an active context in order to be completed. It operates on initiative, along the fringes and indirectly, allowing people to see, experience, and live the square differently. This affords people the ability to position themselves differently in regard to the square by the effects of this ever changing structure and to still receive the benefits of the light and shade provided.

Besides the responsive behavior based on sensors and the air compressor as actuator of the system, a key element that leaves the project open for completion is the use of a soft fabric for the large shading petals. The soft fabric is shaped by the air pumped into it by the compressors but is also formed by the wind. In this way, despite the compressor being numerically controlled, it does not control the form of the petal as it manifests itself in any given moment. The resulting form is an interplay between what the compressor-based mechanism does and the climatic conditions of the moment. The use of this soft cloth, together with air to shape it, was a choice by the architects. They could have chosen a more rigid structure for the petals to more closely control the form of Warde, but instead they opted for a material that they formed through its shape and the way it fills with air but that is also shaped by its environment, mimicking a piece of clothing that is appropriated when worn by a person.

Warde is a structure that takes initiative by itself, conditioned by changes it picks up in its surroundings. And in this way, it amplifies what happens around it.

### Timing and Agency: Awareness of Time Ensures the Relevance of Actions

Warde acts at a fast pace. Its response to others' actions happens instantly, in real time. Petals inflate when pedestrians approach and when the trams arrive at the square's station. They deflate when pedestrians move away. Despite the complexity of its behavior, which arises from the presence of multiple people simultaneously as well as its interplay with climatic conditions such as wind, Warde reacts to the situation in the moment. It provides shade when there is sun and light in the dark, and it acknowledges the presence of others through its behavior. It is moved by people, and it moves people. Through this, it becomes an active member of the public square and contributes to the liveliness of the square. Its opening and closing become an animated dance in the square. It is an animation. It animates the square. It continuously reshapes the square and how the square appears to its visitors.

Through the animation that is conditioned by activities that fill the square, Warde becomes an amplifier of the rhythm of that very square. Warde makes visible the different intensities of flows of people at different times of the day. It makes visible the coming and going of the trams that cut through the square. It also makes visible the wind conditions at any point in time. Warde, in this sense, becomes a technology, as described by Lefebvre, that supports the observation of different kinds of rhythms in the square, and it contributes to this mix of integrated cadences its own rhythm as well.

## Understanding in Action: Forms of Action Are Understood in the Making

Warde makes visible the changes it detects in its surroundings. It makes urban rhythm perceivable, and by doing so, these rhythms can be understood. It is a kind of rhythmanalytic tool built right inside the context of which it amplifies the rhythm. It provides a form of accountability through its form of operation. Warde's reflection of arriving trams becomes a cue that is physically manifest in the larger square and that becomes architectural.

Warde morphs into shading structures through a physical reconfiguration of its petals. While quick, this operation still does take some time. It is a gesture akin to a person lifting and opening an umbrella. You know at the onset of the action what is about to happen. Similarly, Warde's behavior can be anticipated.

As Warde picks up on pedestrian movement, it allows for play and for playful interaction when people get closer and farther away from it. There is a temptation to figure out how this kind of structure works. You see this mostly in children, who start to run around it to see what it does, change their behavior, and observe again, trying to figure out patterns of behavior and trying to figure out what makes it work and if they can control it.

Unexpected Interactions: Interactions Themselves
Are Other than Expected

Warde has a life of its own. It is unpredictable because of the multiple interactions that happen in parallel. Complexity arises on the basis of such multiple elements interacting in parallel. Warde's behavior is necessarily complex, as it is conditioned by multiple elements, all of which change independently and unexpectedly: the wind, the sun, people's movements, and the arriving and departing trains. This complexity makes it more unpredictable than its preprogrammed air-compressor sequences would suggest. Its otherness comes from allowing the wind to condition that preprogrammed behavior.

Warde's unpredictability occurs within a framework of constraints. The system is essentially programmed to inflate petals when a pedestrian presence is detected and when trams approach the station. In that sense, the control system is an action-reaction mapping. The elements of openness and other improvisation-like characteristics described earlier do, however, illustrate how such a controlled and scripted reaction can be complicated by introducing additional degrees of freedom, such as the free movement of the fabric and the complex response to the presence of more than one pedestrian.

## SLOTHBOTS

Unlike the Warde project, the large, autonomous, and box-like robotic monoliths called Slothbots move only very slowly within one of the public areas of a building lobby. Their position and orientation change imperceptibly, and they move in response to the activity of passersby within the space. The Slothbots project was developed by Michael Phillips and Guido Bugman as part of Plymouth University's i-DAT program. It is an experimental project, at the intersection of art and design for public spaces. Slothbots do not have any declared purpose or function but rather examine public life in environments where physical elements such as walls cease to be a static backdrop but become animated, capable of responsively reconfiguring space through movement, and where this responsiveness becomes manifest not in the quickness typically associated with interactive technologies but rather with a slowness more akin to the permanence of the built environment.

Implemented as a prototype in a building lobby, Slothbots pick up on the use of the space they are in and how that space changes throughout the day. They reposition themselves in response to and in anticipation of new interactions with building occupants. By doing so, "they reconfigure the physical architecture over time as a result of their interactions with people."[14]

Slothbots operate using a camera system installed at their location that monitors pedestrian movements as well as Slothbots' locations, and Slothbots' control program runs from an integrated computer linked to a Rug Warrior board built around a microcontroller.

Along with the change in use of the space throughout the day, the Slothbots reposition themselves in anticipation of new interactions with building occupants.

### Open Beginnings: Design for Initiative Ensures Openness

The spatial configurations generated by Slothbots are characterized by an openness that is continuously negotiated between their responsive physical and mobile structure, the human constituents of the space, and the architecture of the space, as

Figure 8. Slothbots, slow-moving, autonomous box structures that continuously reconfigure space conditioned by people's behavior. (Project and photos by i-DAT)

these components condition and reflect each other's behavior. These three components make up the project's *field of possibilities*. As they shift in relation to each other, the Slothbots continuously become something new. Slothbots consider the history of movements as well as in-the-moment moves, which brings in the past of the place as a further element in this relation.

The monolithic wall-like structure is an important component of the Slothbots' openness. The shape of the Slothbots is essentially underspecified. There are no indications whatsoever in regard to the large and tall wall panels that make up the monolith. Uses could conceivably include affixing event posters, which would then make their rounds with Slothbots in the public space, direct writing on the panels, or affixing other elements to clip on objects.

Slothbots are designed for initiative as they move about in the space occupied and offer themselves for integration. They are proactive as objects through their autonomous movement. Imagining Slothbots to have the same form but not be moving autonomously would still maintain all other elements of their physical appearance. However, their manual use would require a deliberate consideration of their utility at first before rolling them to a new location. Instead, operated the way they are, Slothbots offer themselves to be integrated into an activity on their own account.

As part of people's interactions with Slothbots over time, the project continuously generates new meanings. Every interaction discloses something about the project's nature, but these disclosures will never exhaust themselves. Furthermore, every interaction and every use that is made of the Slothbots will change the perception of Slothbots by others. Every interaction will become part of what the Slothbots are seen as and will expand the awareness of the field of possibilities. The Slothbots can be seen as a project that grows on people and their place over time.

### Timing and Agency: Awareness of Time Ensures the Relevance of Actions

Where, when, and how the Slothbots move emerge out of the interaction with building residents and the physical context. The moves involve no plan as such but rather a *protocol* of constraints that, together with people's behavior, results in the movement being constantly conceived as it is enacted. In this way, Slothbots engage and adapt to the constantly changing use that people make of the space they are placed in. They remain relevant to the building and the activities they facilitate.

What stands out as distinctive in the Slothbots project in regard to time, however, is that they move extremely slowly. This slowness stands out in the discourse on improvisation, as that more commonly relates to in-the-moment responsiveness. The Slothbots' latency in response is distinctly beyond real time if we consider the definition given earlier as "the actual time during which a process or event occurs," the processes here being events of human activity. Given that Slothbots live in the public space of a building, the other temporal dimension to consider is that of the building itself. With this consideration, we broaden our understanding of the temporal dimension from the human activity to what, in Lefebvre's terms, we could call the *rhythm of the building*. Slothbots do not in fact engage in real time with the building residents and visitors. They do so, however, much more closely with the temporal scale of the built environment. Walls may see posters being affixed, tables and chairs may be moved aside at the end of the day, windows and doors may be locked for the evening, or hallways may get refurbished for a new term. Similarly, Slothbots engage as a built structure with the long-term usage of the space they reside in, changing orientation and position over the course of hours, days, and weeks.

Slothbots, in their distinct slowness, are therefore a significant pointer toward a temporal dimension of responsiveness that is often overlooked: a temporal scale that is contemplated by Lefebvre's rhythmanalysis as part of the multitude of rhythms that come together in forming a place.

### Understanding in Action: Forms of Action Are Understood in the Making

Slothbots, in their unplanned moves, may block passages, divide space, direct and facilitate flow, or do otherwise. These meanings are attributed as they emerge from the interplay between people, their activities, and the Slothbots, rather than being pre-scribed. Slothbots allow for their behavior to be interpreted and integrated dynamically into people's activities. They do so despite not showing any of the characteristics described in chapter 5 in regard to this position. Slothbots do not give any cues about what they will do next and where they are headed; neither are their moves accountable in any particular way except for in-person observation on site and over long periods of time.

The understanding of *what Slothbots do* happens because they do it slowly. As any of their moves and changes in orientation happen at a speed barely perceptible to human observers, they effectively give cues and become predictable in their moves. Chances are that they will be about where you see them now for the time being. Their slowness gives people time to do *something with* them at any time they encounter them in any one of their unique positions. Even though any position and orientation is transient, its duration is long enough to make sense of it in the context of the situation in which one encounters it. Slothbots, paradoxically and despite their being in motion, are an example of *permanence* as an opportunity for improvisation.

### Unexpected Interactions: Interactions Themselves Are Other than Expected

Slothbots, as an object, cannot be controlled. A set of param-eters conditions their movements, which are context specific, but beyond that, they are literally *out of control*. Their moves are unplanned, unforeseeable, and only contained by the physical boundaries of the space. They are wild things, and, were they to move faster, that would become even more apparent. Instead, they are wildness that unfolds slowly, like creeping vines that take over a terrain when left unattended.

The effect of this ongoing process of regeneration is remark-able, as it results in a continuous novelty bestowed on a space that might otherwise seem familiar. Come back to the same space, and the Slothbots will be somewhere else, posing a different chal-lenge and opportunity for passersby.

Slothbots offer openings for otherness also because of an inbuilt *redundancy* at their material and formal level: they are four relatively large wall panels. The size and volume of Slothbots are substantially bigger than need be for the technology they are operated by. Instead, Slothbots' creators made them deliberately big and bare of any shape that would prescribe a purpose to these large block-like monolithic structures. They are underspecified as objects, like a piece of wall in the middle of a room with no apparent purpose. Because they are these bare, block-like structures, Slothbots are open for people to do with them what is inherently beyond what the makers could have foreseen. They are walls, a canvas if you will, in space that bring themselves into that very space in ever new ways and angles. Slothbots offer to redefine their purpose of being there with any new interaction.

# 7 IMPROVISATION AS TECHNIQUE AND PRACTICE FOR DESIGN

The more original a discovery, the more obvious it seems afterwards.

—ARTHUR KOESTLER, *The Act of Creation*

## IMPROVISATION IN DESIGN PRACTICE

Design has looked at improvisation for some time. The predominant focus in these explorations has been on scenario development. The interactions and behaviors that invest a product or system are difficult to anticipate by a single designer or design team. The complex interactions that emerge between participants during unscripted and unplanned scenario improvisation offer the possibility of unexpected twists and turns for the design process. Improvisation, in this case, helps to increase the pool of considered interactions that any artifact or system may be involved in.

Participatory design methods use improvisation to develop applications in collaboration with users. They attempt to unlock tacit kinds of knowing and gain firsthand appreciation of existing or future conditions by engaging participants and designers together in a concrete situation. In *role-play* techniques, for example, cards are handed to each participant that introduce the scene and contain information about rules associated with that specific scene, goals to be achieved, and the roles that participants enact.[1]

The *design props* technique leverages improvisation that takes place in the everyday context of participants. Participants are provided prototypes of newly conceived artifacts—design props—

that are often projected for future use. Participants are asked to imagine uses for these novel objects during their regular daily routines and to document those uses.[2]

Similar to the design props technique, *cultural probes* or *design probes* are a form of participatory design that leverages improvisation in everyday situations. Participants receive a small package containing any number of artifacts and tasks that prompt them to integrate specific actions into their daily routine and to then record their thoughts, feelings, and reactions associated with these prompts. The objective of these probes is to gain insight into people's values, thoughts, and emotions that occur during their habitual setting and activities while minimally changing these habitual situations.[3]

Beyond the development of user scenarios, improvisation is employed to facilitate the design practice of designers and design teams. It is used to foster a process of creative collaboration, specifically supporting spontaneous contributions to the design work in teams and facilitating the acceptance of mistakes and errors as constructive parts in the collaborative process. For example, a group drawing process in which each participant adds a stroke to a paper without any goal being defined up front becomes a simulation of the risk of "feature creep" in product-development processes. The exercise becomes a training in observing and evaluating the contributions made by others and the attentive consideration of these contributions when adding one's own mark. An exercise called "what are you doing?" creates a forced dissonance between an activity that participants are asked to carry out and another activity that they are asked to describe in words to an audience. The setup deliberately facilitates failure in front of an audience, and the audience in the exercise is asked to applaud in support and embrace such moments of failure constructively. The objective is to familiarize participants with making contributions to group work without suffering from a fear of failure.[4]

In all these cases, improvisation is applied either to the design practice or to the construction of use scenarios for product development. While the improvisation of new use scenarios leverages the unscripted and open nature of the improvisational technique for the construction of scenarios, such scenarios, once improvised, typically are transformed into scripts. These scripts are generated by an improvised process but then become the documented reference for the design process moving forward. With few exceptions, improvisational techniques are not typically applied directly to inform the design of the behavior of artifacts and systems, which, instead, is the key aspect of the improvisation-based design model presented here.

## IMPROVISING THINGS AND SYSTEMS

The discussion thus far has illustrated how the positions of the improvisation-based design model can be employed to analyze existing projects as presented in chapter 6. How, then, can this model be instrumentalized and inform the design of new responsive systems and environments?

Improvisational performers use a rich variety of methods and techniques in their training and practice. These frameworks of practice approach improvisation from different angles and with different emphases. As a common trait, however, they consist in principles, reflections, and exercises through which performers train and hone their ability to listen, to become aware of their environment, and to act productively in response to the moment and to the situation at hand. These frameworks of practice and training offer a rich resource for the design process.

I suggest working with these techniques not to inform the collaborative design practice as such but, rather, to design systems with traits of improvisational behavior on their own, so that systems and artifacts become capable of taking on improvised and improvising roles and in order to facilitate human improvisation in their interactions. As performers practice their improvisation skills, these techniques can inform a method that guides the definition of characteristics in the design of responsive systems, objects, and environments.

Improvisation is practiced in a variety of domains including music, dance, and theater. Some techniques of improvisation focus on language and narrative, other forms work with voice and instruments, and still others involve the whole body in movement and physical interaction. For the design of interactions in urban environments, *movement improvisation* as a form of *performance improvisation* is a particularly good fit.[5] It shares many aspects with the condition of being, as a person, in a city, surrounded by and immersed in the hustle and bustle of people walking and moving in physical space, interacting with each other and with their environment in word, gesture, and motion. Movement improvisation includes a number of specific improvisational practices that focus on creating movement that involves the whole human body: large, all-encompassing motions as well as small, detailed gestures enacted by parts of the body, physical interaction between participants, and interactions with the physical environment of a place. It involves the human actor in a way that is quite similar to ambient interactions of everyday experience and as such provides ample material for the design of urban interactions. In practice, performers of movement improvisation move their bodies in space; they encounter other performers, audience, and objects, constantly changing their spatial conditions. They walk, they see, they talk—the process is akin to the complex dynamics encountered and constructed every day by de Certeau's *Wandersmänner* as they experience the city in its most elementary form: through walking. "Their story begins on ground level, with footsteps. They are myriad, but do not compose a series. They cannot be counted because each unit has a qualitative character: a style of tactile apprehension and kinesthetic singularities. Their intertwined paths give their shape to spaces. They weave places together. In that respect, pedestrian movements form one of the 'real systems whose existence in fact makes up the city.' "[6]

**VIEWPOINTS TECHNIQUE**

In chapter 1, I introduced Viewpoints as an improvisation technique that is of particular interest to the argument developed in these chapters. The technique was formalized and documented by

Anne Bogart, who describes Viewpoints as "a philosophy translated into a technique for (1) training performers; (2) building ensemble; and (3) creating movement for the stage."[7]

Originally developed in the 1970s by Mary Overlie, Viewpoints offers an alternative to conventional approaches to acting, directing, and playwriting. It represents a defined procedure and attitude that is nonhierarchical, practical, and collaborative in nature. It overcomes the often-found dynamic in acting in which directors *want actors to do certain things* ("I want for you to come in and walk across the stage like this," etc.). Instead, Viewpoints focuses on engaging actors as co-creators in the collaborative process of collectively making choices onstage and at the moment of performance. In Bogart's terms, the choices are made in response to *what the play wants,* which we can paraphrase for our context as *what the situation wants.* It is a process in which acting is experienced as a collective discovery of acts that dynamically and recursively respond to the questions that arise (or *emerge*). Viewpoints is based on the "trust in letting something occur onstage, rather than making it occur. The source for action and invention comes to us from others and from the physical world around us."[8]

Viewpoints improvisation is also a training method for performers. In Viewpoints sessions, a trainer works with the performers in gradually building up their capabilities by guiding their attention and adding layers of complexity as input to their behavior. Because Viewpoints performers are so attuned to the space and the moment they inhabit, they are ideal explorers of the potential of a given space and situation. When working toward a specific performance, Viewpoints-trained performers will frequently explore a theatrical set with Viewpoints exercises in order to enlarge the range of possibilities of the set in a more intuitive, explorative, and creative way than can be typically achieved by conventional, director-initiated, top-down staging work.[9]

In Viewpoints improvisation, individual and collective activity emerges in real time, on the basis of actors' heightened awareness and immediate response to any of nine viewpoints that are temporal and spatial in nature: tempo, duration, kinesthetic response, and repetition are the four temporal viewpoints; spatial relationship, topography, shape, gesture, and architecture are the five spatial viewpoints. In improvisation training, these viewpoints are introduced one at a time, inviting actors to practice awareness of and attention to each viewpoint separately as they develop their movement and actions. Gradually, the viewpoints are combined, layered, and engaged with simultaneously, developing complex dynamics of interaction. A Viewpoints coach can facilitate the process and guide actors' awareness to any one or any combination of viewpoints in their work.

When using Viewpoints as a design method, each of the viewpoints that performers use to dynamically engage with their environment represents a potentially constitutive element for the description of the behavior of responsive artifacts and environments. As Viewpoints performers focus on one viewpoint at a time to craft their behavior and their response to a situation, so can designers and architects use these viewpoints to articulate and define the behavioral traits of the system or environments they design to engage with the situation at hand.

## Temporal Viewpoints

*Tempo* is concerned with how fast or slow an action is. It does not matter what the action is; it explores extremes of tempo—very fast and very slow—together with the medium and guides the attention to meaning created by the tempo of an action (slow to touch or fast to grab, etc.). It brings awareness to the inner and outer tempo of a performer, remaining calm inside while acting fast, and vice versa, or engaging in fast collective action while keeping a slow pace at an individual level.

*Duration* works on an awareness of how long an action lasts, developing a sense for how long is long enough to make something happen or how long is too long so that something starts to die. Again, it explores the extremes as areas from which we tend to shy away—something that lasts too long or too short—while intuitively retreating toward a medium comfort zone. Viewpoints improvisation willingly pushes beyond those behavioral comfort zones to make something happen.

*Kinesthetic response* brings attention to other bodies in space, to their movements, and asks the performer to explore one's own behavior as being impacted by these external mobilities. The focus is now on when you move instead of how fast or slow or for how long you move. The focus here is "the immediate, uncensored response to an external event around you."[10]

*Repetition* is perhaps the viewpoint that most directly connects to the discourse of improvisation in a systems perspective. With the focus on this viewpoint, performers experiment with letting when, how, and for how long they move be determined by repetition. Performers may focus on repeating someone else—someone close or someone far—or repeating two people simultaneously. Performers experiment with repetition over time, recycling movements carried out by others in the near or distant past, reproducing forms and figures, and repurposing them for interactions in that moment.

## Spatial Viewpoints

*Spatial relationship* works on the distance between performers and between bodies in motion. Performers examine taking distance from others, getting close, closer, and then too close. They experience dynamic distance and its effects, not dissimilar from what we discussed earlier in regard to the Japanese concept of *hyoshi*.

*Topography* brings attention to the shape within which performers move. Several exercises are based on movements along an imaginary grid. This grid gets changed, broken, and distorted. Performers are asked to imagine and become aware of boundaries within which they move. They move on imaginary three-dimensional grids, painting shapes on the floor with their movement; they work with shape, size of playing space, and patterns within that space. As viewpoints are combined, topography is, for example, explored in fast and slow tempo, triggering different shapes to emerge.

*Shape* is created by the group of performers following an input from the coach or emerging out of free collective movement, with performers becoming aware of lines and curves in how performers are configured in space. Performers train their awareness on the legibility of those shapes both from within the ensemble and from outside. Shapes in space and in motion of this kind are held constant over time and through continuous slow or fast or even increasing tempo of movement. Shapes might dissolve, and performers experiment with changing location within a shape or trigger novel shapes through their action.

*Gesture* is explored by investigating behavioral and expressive gestures. The former are derived from social interactions (pointing, waving, saluting, scratching, etc.), while the latter relate to the interior (expressing feeling, desire, an idea, or a value). Bogart and Landau refer to them as either prosaic or poetic.

*Architecture,* as a viewpoint, works with the spatial qualities that are already present at the site of performance. Performers put attention on how the awareness of the physical environment affects their movement and their behavior. They enter into a dialogue with a room, a space, to let movement evolve out of the surroundings. Architecture is broken down into five further domains: solid mass (walls, floors, doors, furniture, windows, etc.), texture (the material composition of the solid masses), light (the source of it as well as the shadows it casts, etc.), color (of solid mass objects but also light), sound (what is created directly from the architecture, e.g., from feet walking on different surfaces, creaking of a door, etc.). Performers also work with objects within that space, to create with and through these objects.

## DESIGNING IMPROVISING URBAN APPLICATIONS

Equipped with a better understanding of the technique and the nature of the individual viewpoints, the following example illustrates how the Viewpoints technique of improvisation can be used to support the design of a concrete urban application. For this example, we will look at a system for responsive street lighting and develop its behavior with the help of a number of viewpoints and in relation to the four key positions of the improvisation-based design model.

Today, the integration of LED, sensing, and network technologies is enabling street lighting systems to be responsive to environmental conditions but also to human presence and activity. Street lights can be controlled individually in relation to context-related demand, offering in this way an enticing opportunity to address issues related to urban energy consumption and light pollution. Although working prototypes of such systems do exist, the design of the behavior of these light systems is not straightforward because street lighting touches on manifold issues, such as general visibility, way finding, exploration, active and social use of outdoor spaces, and safety.[11] A common approach for the behavior of such responsive systems holds to a "light follows people" notion, activating or modulating street lights as a reaction to locally detected human presence. Although feasible, this approach appears limiting. In the "light follows people" approach, the *visible city* becomes reduced to one's own immediate presence alone, raising questions related to more visibility farther ahead, visibility for exploration, and visibility for the choice of ad hoc paths.

Let us turn to Viewpoints improvisation to see how this technique can inform the design of responsive urban lighting by developing a lighting behavior that goes beyond the "light follows people" approach.

Experimenting with viewpoint *repetition* in the context of responsive urban lighting offers a number of design possibilities. The light path, formed by individually controlled light posts, can follow a pedestrian, repeating his or her path in real time. However, it also can repeat these paths at later moments, triggered by other pedestrians, illuminating traces of past activity and so forming an invitation to explore unexpected paths.

Looking at the viewpoint *tempo* in relation to responsive urban lighting, any light path activates in a certain way, one lamp at a time, so that a sense of motion and of tempo is conveyed.[12] This unfolding of a light path can be slow or fast; it can reflect the rhythm of the walker or contrast with it, leading to questions of how different tempos of light might feed back and condition people's walking itself.

For urban lighting, the viewpoint *duration* leads to experimentation with how long a light path stays lit—whether it dims as soon as a pedestrian leaves the light cone or whether it stays lit until she or he turns the corner.

For *kinesthetic response* in the context of the lighting application, the bodies in space involved directly are people and lighting fixtures, and the development of lighting behavior can be based on the dynamic proximity between these two. The intensity of a light can increase as a person comes close, reflecting the impact of a passerby. Walking along a lit path then changes from experiencing an evenly lit space to one in which one's own movement translates into rhythmic waves of light, quite naturally reflecting and anticipating one's own way of moving through space—a gentle pulse conditioned by people's movements.

At this point, the work with four viewpoints has helped generate a number of dynamic behavioral sketches. Work with the other five viewpoints can be done in a similar way, and this work of course can be developed in greater depth. Some of these viewpoints-based light behaviors might then be combined, increasing the complexity of the overall system behavior.

The behavior of this improvisational urban light system is now notably different from its original static or reactive version, and an examination through the lens of the four positions presented earlier shows how. Its behavior embodies how *design for initiative ensures openness,* in that the behavior of the light system and that of people are mutually constitutive. Both people and lighting system have agency for taking the first step, and this provides openings for people to participate in the production of urban light. Any change in how people move in space conditions how light is modulated, and this change in light opens possibilities for a change in people's behavior and paths. The system is open but not arbitrary because the behavior structures developed through the work with Viewpoints improvisation frame the field of possibilities, determining a focus of attention and awareness of the system.

In this system, *awareness of time ensures the relevance of actions,* in that the way and tempo at which a person engages with an emerging light path becomes a constitutive part of the timing of the interaction between person and lighting system. Timing becomes paramount, and meaning is attributed to an unpredictable lighting behavior by the way a person engages with it in the here and now. Observing the city at a specific place and lit in a certain way at any one moment becomes a unique opportunity for an observer to engage in an exploration possible only at that moment. If engaged, the light will follow along in some way; otherwise, that moment and its light condition will pass.

*Forms of action are understood in the making,* in that a person observes and interprets light paths, anticipating an upcoming form of these paths simultaneously as they unfold. At the same time, a person's path also is picked up and interpreted by the system. Changes in path direction are interpreted to anticipate a future path and are used to determine lighting behavior. Cues that point to upcoming behaviors become critical. For example, the pulsating light developed through the viewpoint of kinesthetic response becomes indexical in that its appearance points to a specific situation that generates it. The pulsating light paths, as they unfold, feed into the interaction with the passersby. At times, these anticipated behavioral forms correspond to subsequent actions; at other times, these expectations will not be fulfilled. Such misunderstandings are welcome and an integral part of the improvisational nature of this interaction; they are the noise that leads to the emergence of novel behavior, both by the people and by the lighting system.

These *interactions themselves are other than expected,* because while the behavior of this lighting system is conditioned by people's behavior, its functioning can neither be fully understood nor controlled. The lighting system never quite repeats the same behavior, and interactions between people and the lighting system are unpredictable and do not cease to surprise. The result is an urban environment whose lighting conditions are in constant flux.

With the changing light, the city appears to the observing by-stander in ever changing ways.

What an improvising urban light system does is offer a way to reduce the energy consumed by urban street lighting compared to always-on systems. However, it does so without collapsing the city's visual presence and availability to the sole location of the urban observer, as happens with "light follows people" systems. An improvisation-based modality of interaction, as outlined, enables a nighttime illumination of a city that is akin to the unique-ness and liveliness of light conditions generated by daylight illu-mination and its interplay of reflections, refractions, and shadings. Furthermore, it opens up the possibility for people's direct par-ticipation in the behavior of an urban environment without falling back into reactive and repetitive patterns.

Viewpoints improvisation is particularly indicated to be em-ployed for an improvisation-based design approach for responsive urban environments given the proximity of some of its viewpoints with key aspects of established practices in architecture and inter-action design. Viewpoints such as tempo and duration are habit-ual aspects of attention for interaction designers, as are gesture, spatial relationship, and shape. The viewpoints topography and architecture are, of course, the focus of the latter's namesake do-main and guide the attention toward how constructed physical environments are experienced by humans aesthetically.

In similar ways, other techniques and frameworks of impro-visation, such as Action Theater, founded by the director and performer Ruth Zaporah, or Contact Improvisation, developed in the early 1970s by the dancer and choreographer Steve Paxton, bear the potential to be employed to inform the design of the behavior of responsive urban environments in hybrid cities.

## PERFORMANCE-BASED DESIGN IN THE CITY AS CLASSROOM

Some of my recent work with architecture and design students provided an opportunity to experiment with some of the impro-visation-based principles espoused in this book. The scope of the work bridges different scales, ranging from local observations and interventions at the scale of a sidewalk and a public square to systemic considerations at the scale of a street, a neighborhood, or a city.

Short design exercises on a small and local scale provide an opportunity to work with improvisation- and performance-related notions and concepts in the design work before tackling larger contexts at the scale of a neighborhood or a city. One of these short exercises is a twenty-minute observational study—followed by a twenty-minute design charrette—that takes inspiration from Michel de Certeau's *Walking in the City*.[13] During the first part, we observe people walking across nearby public spaces such as a public square or a section of a sidewalk. Participants in the exercise are prompted to recall de Certeau's emphasis on the quality of walking in the city and to develop a rich description of their observations visually and in writing. The attention is guided toward questions such as, Who walks across this place? Where do people look? What do they observe? Who do they interact with? Do they cut corners, take shortcuts, or do something unexpected? Do they change their mind and change paths? I ask participants to map people's paths but most importantly to describe the quality of the walks they observe.

On the basis of the observation of people's walks across the square, participants then begin the twenty-minute design charrette with the goal to *redesign a place through performative interventions*. I ask participants to redesign the public space they just observed without making any or only few physical changes but instead by developing performative interventions. As an inspiration, I point them to the case described in Christopher Dell and Ton Matton's "Improvisation Technology as Mode of Redesigning the Urban," which discusses the project of Place Leon Aucoc in Bordeaux, developed by the Paris-based architects Lacaton and Vassal. The architects, in carrying out the project, "approached the site by entering the situation itself—spending time in the square. They realized that structurally the square already had everything that was needed. Therefore, they did not believe physical changes were appropriate."[14] This observation, however, did not lead Lacaton and Vassal to conclude that nothing ought to be done. "Instead [of making physical changes] we drew up a catalogue of maintenance measures which were strikingly obvious and yet completely neglected, including regularly cleaning the place of dog excrements in order to make it possible to play the game of pétanque on it once again."[15] In doing so, the architects inverted the design approach and held off making any physical additions at all. "By dealing with the square in a performative way, they improved its usability—what is done with the square, how it is used—and thus stimulated the neighborhood, activated it."[16] The approach to the redesign of the square that Lacaton and Vassal pursued leveraged the potential of the square that was already present but unseen. Their work became an uncovering of a background in front of which everyday activities could play out more authentically.

Participants in the design charrette were prompted with these considerations, and on the basis of their previous observations, they developed performative interventions by making no or only minor physical changes while focusing on the *behavior* of the square itself, on its visible or invisible *potential*. For example, they observed how large planters along a square hindered pedestrian flow but at the same time became attractors, as people used the edges to sit, alone or in company. The extensive green space inside the planters, however, seemed underutilized. Participants felt that the space could be made useful by making it accessible for people to lie and linger on. The planter edges could be maintained as they are and offer seating but be opened up at some points to allow access to the green spaces inside the planters. By loosening up the vegetation and adding a layer of grass, these planters could become welcoming places to socialize and to relax. At a slightly higher level than the ground plane where people walk by, these accessible planters would be prime spots to sit and observe the busy walkers across the square.

Another proposal was based on an attentive observation of the proximity of an art gallery located in an adjacent building of the observed square. The location of this gallery is somewhat hidden and tricky to reach despite being so close to the busy square. This observation led students to accentuate the proximity by suggesting a virtual presence of the art gallery in the square. By means of a graphic mark on the pavement of the square, an area would be designated to be a virtual outpost of the gallery and could be curated and used for performances on demand. By locating part of the programming of the gallery right in the outdoor square, a virtual connection between the busy and animated square and the gallery would be created. With the two locations being connected, people coming by the square would be exposed to an invitation to seek out the gallery, and visitors in the gallery would be made aware of the outdoor extension of the exhibition space. This ad hoc stage-like zone could be used by the gallery for real-time projections and performances related to ongoing activities at the gallery.

Last but not least, one proposal focused on the seasonal nature of life in the square, given that the day of observation was a rather cold fall day. Cold and wet or snowy weather was observed as reducing the willingness for people to slow down in the square to engage with others. Some participants observed that walkers carrying warm coffee or tea cups walked slower than others did. Participants contemplated extreme weather situations such as thick layers of snow during winter months and responded to this condition in a performative way, proposing to make snow-shoveling tools available in the square during winter. The idea would be to make snow shoveling a fun activity for passersby to build their own snow structures and sculptures, such as seats, fortifications, snow bars, and so on. To lift the moods during chilly weather, a small mobile tea and coffee cart was proposed. In this proposal, the designers did not choose to alleviate or control a condition of discomfort but instead proposed to work with the condition of discomfort in a productive way: if it is snowy and cold, then let's use this to build something together!

These exercises are warmups to experiment with improvisation-based and performative design approaches and prepare for more comprehensive work in larger contexts such as a recent work with graduate students that I began in 2018 that focuses on Boston's Columbia Road and that we are developing in collaboration with the Cambridge-based advocacy group LivableStreets Alliance. This research work explores ways in which to enhance Columbia

Road's experience for residents and visitors beyond its current emphasis as a transportation artery.

In this work, the 2.3-mile-long Columbia Road is the context of investigation. The street connects Franklin Park and Joe Moakley Park as well as the waterfront in South Boston. It represents the missing link of the Emerald Necklace (Boston's public park system) between these two parks as originally envisioned by Frederick Law Olmsted. Columbia Road is today an integral part of a series of diverse neighborhoods and communities. It fulfills essential urban connections but points in many ways also to a lack in the network of urban spaces, representing opportunities for change. The street is considered a priority project for the city of Boston and part of the early action group in the "Imagine Boston 2030" initiative.

Together with our project partners, we identified a number of sites along the street that appear to be underutilized and that are either a property of the city of Boston or of entities that have a strong public interest.

The work with the graduate students involves a research phase including observational studies and conversations with members of local communities to become familiar with and get a better understanding of the context. On the basis of this research, the proposals for interventions use individual or combinations of some of the identified underutilized spaces. And they bridge interventions that can be material or immaterial, involve objects, services, information systems, ambient installations, events, and the like, or any combination of these. We look at Columbia Road as a place of possibilities, of participation and co-creation; a place of destination, of transit, and of retreat; a place for encounter, of connection, of proximity, and of distance; and a place for dynamic appropriation where meaning is negotiated as part of an ongoing interaction between people and place.

A reference in this work is David Brown's Available City project, which I briefly mentioned in chapter 4.[17] Brown leverages the city of Chicago's ownership of fifteen thousand vacant lots through organizational interventions using improvisation techniques to become catalyzing agents for the production of a new system of public spaces. As described before, Available City proposes a sophisticated set of rules that involves private developers in constructing interventions on up to five adjacent or disconnected lots that can each be developed vertically as long as access to a public space of equal size to the original lot is maintained. The production of public space in this model happens not on the basis of an a priori plan but rather as an ongoing application of a framework for interactions between citizens, developers, the city, and other stakeholders in the development of underutilized city-owned lots. The key contribution of the project is a set of new relationships that facilitate the generation of shared value on previously underutilized public land. Through the application of these relational rules, the design process becomes an iterative continuum, a continuous process of redesign that is open for initiative by diverse groups of stakeholders, in which the effectiveness of any intervention depends on the timing related to all other interventions and that is capable of generating unexpected outcomes. Available City is an ongoing improvisation of the generation of public space, as part of which stakeholders respond to as well as construct a dynamic situation through each of their choices.

In creating proposals for the underutilized spaces along Columbia Road, we work with these kinds of improvisational design frameworks at an organizational as well as material and informational level. The objective is to construct interventions that in constructive ways remain open, relevant, and resilient for the changes that will involve the street and its neighborhoods in the years to come.

## DESIGNER AS COACH

So far, work with improvisation in the context of design and architecture has largely focused on collaborative work practices between designers and the generation of use scenarios.

In the context of the hybrid city, the central design focus is increasingly shifting toward the behavior of designed systems due to their responsive and interactive nature. In the context of software design, the so-called look and feel has already been a key issue for some time, but this has been less so the case for interventions at an urban scale.[18]

When the attention turns to the behavior of responsive artifacts and systems in cities, non-script-based performance has an advantage over plan-based or script-based behavior. In this book, improvisation as a concept and as an art has informed the four positions of the improvisation-based design model. Furthermore, the rich landscape of frameworks for improvisational practice and training is yet another way in which we can leverage improvisation in the way we design the behavior of things and systems in the hybrid city.

When working with improvisation techniques, the designer takes on a role somewhat similar to a coach, as in the case of Viewpoints. The designer is not a coach in the work with performers but in the work with designed systems, guiding attention to any one or any combination of viewpoints as dimensions of awareness, sensitivity, and expression when engaging with context and the situation at hand.

In today's context of hybrid cities, the question no longer begins with what technology *can do*. Instead, the questions are about what constitutes meaningful interactions that hybrid city interventions *can facilitate*. The answer to such a question, then, is not any single response. Instead, it is a process that keeps unfolding over time. What is meaningful is what becomes part of an ongoing process of meaning-making in interaction with citizens in ever new and different ways. Improvisational techniques and performance-based approaches to the way we design the behavior of hybrid city environments can guide us in the design process for interventions that remain relevant and significant in the lives of a city and its inhabitants over time.

# 8 EPILOGUE

## Toward the Urban Improvise

To improvise is to welcome the unknown.

—PHILIPPE PETIT, high-wire walker

We have certainly lived through more poetic times in the narration of cities. Embedded sensors, wireless networks, and interactive environments hardly rival the accounts of urban life by the likes of Calvino, Dickens, Joyce, and Proust.

The focus on efficiency, data-driven predictability, and control in the narrative about cities over the past two decades strikingly recalls the early days of the twentieth century. What then was the idealized new and modern has become the smart of today.

The development of technology has long pursued the superlatives of faster, higher, bigger, cleaner, stronger, better, and safer. This was a promising strategy when the scope and reach of technologies were limited. Today, however, networked information technologies pervade not only cities but also large and intricate parts of our everyday practice. Pressing questions now become, efficiency on whose terms? predictability based on what agency? and control by whom? The superlatives of abstraction have given way to the quest for meaning in situations and context.

Experience shows that dismissing technology altogether is not viable and probably not a desirable path. Technology is unlikely to go away. Humans have always lived with technology. While the artificial is often contrasted with the natural, both truly come together within human nature. Technology is not external to human practice but rather an utmost expression of it. Technology is the means for human survival in and adaptation to the environment. Cracking a shell using a rock is a technology. Writing with pen and paper is also a technology. Riding a bicycle equipped with GPS and cellular technology that can be shared with other residents of a city is technology too. Technology is an intrinsic part of being human; it mediates the way we live in this world.

Technology has always been a tool for humans to adapt to nature by keeping under control things that are perceived as dangerous, as a threat, as wild. To create order where there was perceived disorder, to make things predictable, avoiding unfavorable surprise, has always been the promise of technology. Humans have consistently dreaded uncertainty and risk in dealing with their environment. Farming reduced the risk of hunting; houses took away the uncertainty of nomadic tents. Today, an entire industry is dedicated to the desire to reduce risk and uncertainty by selling it off to others.

Plans in various forms have come to be the tool of creating order. Their execution, then, is an expression of the belief in the value and ability of control. Previous technologies have been good at that mode of operation. They often excel at operating according to program, behaving as planned to maintain the prescribed order and reduce uncertainty.

The trouble is that real life keeps being messy, and things do not always work out as planned. Or, as Woody Allen allegedly put it, "If you want to make God laugh, tell him about your plans."[1]

Come to think of it, humans actually do rather well in dealing with unpredictability. The creative act itself defies control and predictability. To make or create something new is an inconceivable coming together of entities and ideas that were thought of as mutually exclusive before. To bring them together defies existing order, rule, and norm; it is somewhat akin to committing a crime, in Philippe Petit's words.[2] Lucy Suchman's work on the situated nature of human actions provided a wakeup call to designers and developers in the later part of the twentieth century on how plans, while valuable documents before and after the action, are less relevant during the action, when we encounter a specific situation.[3] When we adapt to a situation, we work with it; we adjust our initial plan and respond to what the situation demands in the moment—we, ultimately, improvise.

One of humans' quintessential traits is the ability to respond in unique ways to a situation, to take initiative, to take action, to set things in motion at any time and in unexpected ways. To take a step against all odds, as Hannah Arendt argues, that could not have been predicted is to be quintessentially human.[4]

In many ways, cities are the utmost expression of this idea. They attract not because they fulfill people's expectations but because of the assumption that they exceed those expectations. People come to cities for what lies beyond their expectation, for the unforeseen and for the uncertain. There is perceived value in the messiness and in the otherness that is encountered in cities.

Instead of attempting to tame the unplanned, uncontrollable, and wild through the use of data-driven technologies following a design approach based on predictive and probability-based planning, I want to encourage readers to look at these technologies as capable of living in and with a future that remains to be written *in the moment* and that maintains its *potential* and its *openness*.

This book makes a case for working with uncertainty in new, productive ways when we design interactions in hybrid cities. Hybrid city technologies go beyond programmed and planned behavior. They sense context, adapt, and respond to situations with discrimination. In their support of humans in the continuous struggle to adapt to the environment, they can do so beyond fixed notions of control and order. Technology can facilitate situations and in-the-moment interaction, becoming part of a dynamic and inclusive *production of presence*. I argue that we need new design models to disclose this potential better.

Improvisation has been employed as a metaphor for such behavior before, but it has more to offer than that. In this book, I argue that the in-depth exploration of the art and practice of improvisation can inform the way we design interactions for the hybrid city in more substantial ways. In its simultaneity of conception and action and iterative and recursive nature of operating, improvisation is an exceptional domain to tap for how we understand and create interactions between humans and hybrid city environments. The improvisation-based framework presented in this book is the result of my attempt to do this. It is not a normative theory and does not suggest judgment as to good or bad design. In fact, the model is best applied recursively, adopting its own positions toward itself in its application.

In this way, openness is not a simplistic prescription but rather a question, a space to examine possible forms of such openness. As improvisation emphasizes an understanding that unfolds during the course of an action, it points toward the very construction of new ways of such understanding that emerge during and from this process. And, finally, the embrace of otherness in the proposed design model applied toward itself encourages an ongoing questioning of what we consider as other and remaining open to evolving forms of otherness that may also reside within what appears most familiar.

Urban interaction design using an improvisation-based model fosters an awareness that every situation is constructed through direct individual and collective participation. It fosters the bringing in of multiple points of view and diverse positions to continuously complete a work anew in unique ways, in this way maintaining its relevance. A design approach based on improvisation relates, then, to a view of human development that involves participation and growth. Taking on the risk of acting in the moment, of acting without knowing what to expect, of improvising, is fundamentally an attitude toward change and adaptation. It is a turning away from preconceptions and from getting stuck. It is a perspective on human development as a productive commitment to the development of one's own experiential horizons. Design for improvisation focused on openness and initiative assumes a profound ethical dimension of respect for the self and for the other.

In this view, the designer's focus shifts toward ensuring that interventions remain sufficiently open to be adapted to changing circumstances, that an intervention is laid out in a way that enables, invites, and even encourages citizens to take part in shaping the impact it has on their everyday life, and that it does not remain stuck in dynamics that may have lost relevance. An improvisation-based design approach focuses on generating fields of possibilities that foster conversation that is open to diverse and changing forms of participation, that is aware and respectful of conversations that came before, and that is able to accept unexpected and other directions that conversations will take in the future.

The designer, in this process, becomes a facilitator of performance and a mediator. His or her task is nothing less than constructing interventions that perform gracefully in this kind of dynamic and that are capable of remaining relevant despite or because they embrace a notion of situated everyday life that is ultimately out of control for the designer. My hope is that the notions and concepts presented in this book can challenge the way designers and architects think about their work in today's hybrid cities and that they can motivate us to explore a new path for design.

# NOTES

## 1. INTRODUCTION

Epigraph: Italo Calvino, *Invisible Cities* (New York: Harcourt, 1978), 155.

1. Lucy A. Suchman was an early voice to discuss situated action as juxtaposed to planned action. See Suchman, *Plans and Situated Actions: The Problem of Human-Machine Communication* (Cambridge: Cambridge University Press, 1987).

2. Pierre Lévy, in *Becoming Virtual* (New York: Plenum Trade, 1998), extensively discusses processes of virtualization and actualization. His framing of the issue is of particular interest to the design of interactions in today's hybrid city affording numerous opportunities to virtualize everyday processes and activities.

3. A project in this sense was realized in 2010–13 by the author and colleagues at the MIT Senseable City Lab as part of the research initiative LIVE Singapore!

4. An early discussion of this changing condition of the built urban environment can be found in Malcolm McCullough, *Digital Ground: Architecture, Pervasive Computing, and Environmental Knowing* (Cambridge, Mass.: MIT Press, 2005), 47–64.

5. Hugh Dubberly, Paul Pangaro, and Usman Haque make clear distinctions among different kinds of interaction (e.g., reacting, learning, conversing, collaborating, designing) and provide a more rigorous definition of the term that goes beyond its common notions. See Dubberly, Pangaro, and Haque, "What Is Interaction? Are There Different Types?" *Interactions* 16, no. 1 (2009).

6. Michael Batty, "The Computable City," *International Planning Studies* 2 (1997); William J. Mitchell, *City of Bits: Space, Place, and the*

*Infobahn* (Cambridge, Mass.: MIT Press, 1995); Anthony M. Townsend, "The Internet and the Rise of the New Network Cities, 1969–1999," *Environment and Planning B: Planning and Design* 28, no. 1 (2001).

7. Rob Kitchin, "Making Sense of Smart Cities: Addressing Present Shortcomings," *Cambridge Journal of Regions, Economy and Society* 8, no. 1 (2015).

8. "Smarter Planet" was an ad campaign by IBM, launched in 2008 and following a speech by then-CEO Sam Palmisano that announced the term. As part of this campaign, the company developed a number of inspirational graphics and op-eds proclaiming that novel "smart" technology solutions would be able to radically address and solve key global issues.

9. Quotes are from corporate communications by IBM, Living PlanIT, and Siemens and are quoted in Adam Greenfield, *Against the Smart City (the City Is Here for You to Use Book 1)* (Do projects, 2013), loc. 185 of 2470, Kindle, an exhaustive analysis and critique of the claims of technology companies in regard to smart city initiatives.

10. Robert G. Hollands, "Critical Interventions into the Corporate Smart City," *Cambridge Journal of Regions, Economy and Society* 8, no. 1 (2015); Greenfield, *Against the Smart City*.

11. Rob Kitchin, "The Real-Time City? Big Data and Smart Urbanism," *GeoJournal* 79, no. 1 (2014).

12. Ayona Datta, "The Smart Entrepreneurial City: Dholera and 100 Other Utopias in India," in *Smart Urbanism: Utopian Vision or False Dawn?* ed. Simon Marvin, Andrés Luque-Ayala, and Colin McFarlane (New York: Routledge, 2015); Nancy Odendaal, "Getting Smart About Smart Cities in Cape Town: Beyond the Rhetoric," in Marvin, Luque-Ayala, and McFarlane, *Smart Urbanism;* C. Z. Nnaemeka, "The Unexotic Underclass," *MIT Entrepreneurship Review,* May 19, 2013, http://miter.mit.edu/the-unexotic-underclass.

13. Robert G. Hollands, "Beyond the Corporate Smart City? Glimpses of Other Possibilities of Smartness," in Marvin, Luque-Ayala, and McFarlane, *Smart Urbanism;* Rob Kitchin, Tracey P. Lauriault, and Gavin McArdle, "Smart Cities and the Politics of Urban Data," in Marvin, Luque-Ayala, and McFarlane, *Smart Urbanism*.

14. Stéphane Roche, Nashid Nabian, Kristian Kloeckl, and Carlo Ratti, "Are 'Smart Cities' Smart Enough?" in *Spatially Enabling Government, Industry and Citizens: Research and Development Perspectives,* ed. Abbas Rajabifard, and David Coleman (Needham, Mass.: GSDI Association Press, 2012); Paolo Cardullo and Rob Kitchin, "Being a 'Citizen' in the Smart City: Up and Down the Scaffold of Smart Citizen Participation," *GeoJournal,* January 2018; Anthony M. Townsend, *Smart Cities: Big Data, Civic Hackers, and the Quest for a New Utopia* (New York: Norton, 2013), 284.

15. Stephen Goldsmith and Susan Crawford, *The Responsive City: Engaging Communities Through Data-Smart Governance* (San Francisco: Jossey-Bass, 2014).

16. Laura Forlano, "Decentering the Human in the Design of Collaborative Cities," *Design Issues* 32, no. 3 (2016); Marcus Foth, "The Next Urban Paradigm: Cohabitation in the Smart City," *it–Information Technology* 59, no. 6 (2017); Martijn de Waal and Marloes Dignum, "The Citizen in the Smart City: How the Smart City Could Transform Citizenship," *it–Information Technology* 59, no. 6 (2017); Carl DiSalvo and Jonathan Lukens, "Ropocentrism and the Nonhuman in Design: Possibilities for Designing New Forms of Engagement With and Through Technology," in *From Social Butterfly to Engaged Citizen: Urban Informatics, Social Media, Ubiquitous Computing, and Mobile Technology to Support Citizen Engagement*, ed. Marcus Foth, Laura Forlano, Christine Satchell, and Martin Gibbs (Cambridge, Mass.: MIT Press, 2011).

17. An example for an incentive-based behavior compliance can be found in Sunyoung Kim, Jennifer Mankoff, and Eric Paulos, "Sensr: Evaluating a Flexible Framework for Authoring Mobile Data-Collection Tools for Citizen Science," *Proceedings of the 2013 Conference on Computer Supported Cooperative Work*, 2013; Yong Liu, Pratch Piyawongwisal, Sahil Handa, Liang Yu, Yan Xu, and Arjmand Samuel, "Going Beyond Citizen Data Collection with Mapster: A Mobile+ Cloud Real-Time Citizen Science Experiment," e-Science Workshops (eScienceW), 2011.

18. Robert G. Hollands, "Will the Real Smart City Please Stand Up? Intelligent, Progressive or Entrepreneurial," *City* 12, no. 3 (2008).

19. Jennifer Gabrys, *Program Earth: Environmental Sensing Technology and the Making of a Computational Planet* (Minneapolis: University of Minnesota Press, 2016).

20. The term comes from the Hybrid City conference series that was started in 2011 and organized by the University Research Institute of Applied Communication (URIAC) in Athens. Subsequently, a second and third conference were held in 2013 and 2015, respectively.

21. Alan Kay, "User Interface: A Personal View," in *The Art of Human-Computer Interface Design*, ed. Brenda Laurel and Joy S. Mountford (Reading, Mass.: Addison-Wesley, 1990).

22. Gordon Pask, "The Architectural Relevance of Cybernetics," *Architectural Design* 39, no. 9 (1969); Gordon Pask, *Conversation Theory: Applications in Education and Epistemology* (Amsterdam: Elsevier, 1976).

23. Ranulph Glanville, "Researching Design and Designing Research," *Design Issues* 15, no. 2 (1999); Dubberly, Pangaro, and Haque, "What Is Interaction?"

24. Andrew Monk, "Common Ground in Electronically Mediated Communication: Clark's Theory of Language Use," *HCI Models, Theories, and Frameworks: Toward a Multidisciplinary Science*, ed. John M. Carroll

(San Francisco: Morgan Kaufmann, 2003); Herbert H. Clark and Susan E. Brennan, "Grounding in Communication," *Perspectives on Socially Shared Cognition* 13 (1991).

25. Discussions of Aristotle's notion of an agent as being one who takes action (laid out in his *Poetics* and *Metaphysics*) are numerous; my main references are Hannah Arendt, *The Human Condition* (Chicago: University of Chicago Press, 1998), 7–17, 187; and, more specifically in the context of design, Brenda Laurel, *Computers as Theatre* (Upper Saddle River, N.J.: Addison-Wesley, 2013), 71–73; and Richard Buchanan, "Rhetoric, Humanism, and Design," in *Discovering Design*, ed. Richard Buchanan and Victor Margolin (Chicago: University of Chicago Press, 1995).

26. Suchman, *Plans and Situated Actions;* Paul Dourish, *Where the Action Is: The Foundations of Embodied Interaction* (Cambridge, Mass.: MIT Press, 2001); Victor Kaptelinin and Bonnie A. Nardi, *Acting with Technology: Activity Theory and Interaction Design* (Cambridge, Mass.: MIT Press, 2006).

27. Donald Norman, foreword to Laurel, *Computers as Theatre*, xii.

28. Laurel, *Computers as Theatre*, 11.

29. John Rudlin, *Commedia dell'Arte: An Actor's Handbook* (New York: Routledge, 1994); Henning Mehnert, *Commedia dell'Arte* (Stuttgart: Reclam, 2003).

30. Michel de Certeau, *The Practice of Everyday Life* (Berkeley: University of California Press, 2011).

31. Batty, "Computable City," 155.

32. Enrico Moretti, *The New Geography of Jobs* (New York: Mariner Books, 2013).

33. Alfonso Montuori, "The Complexity of Improvisation and the Improvisation of Complexity: Social Science, Art and Creativity," *Human Relations* 56, no. 2 (2003).

34. Edgar Landgraf, *Improvisation as Art: Conceptual Challenges, Historical Perspectives* (London: Bloomsbury Academic, 2014), 16.

35. Landgraf, *Improvisation as Art*, 36.

36. Paul F. Berliner, *Thinking in Jazz: The Infinite Art of Improvisation* (Chicago: University of Chicago Press, 1994), 222; Karl E. Weick, "Introductory Essay—Improvisation as a Mindset for Organizational Analysis," *Organization Science* 9, no. 5 (1998).

37. Montuori, "Complexity of Improvisation," 241; Gary Peters, *The Philosophy of Improvisation* (Chicago: University of Chicago Press, 2012).

38. Mark C. Taylor, *The Moment of Complexity: Emerging Network Culture* (Chicago: University of Chicago Press, 2001).

39. Peter Anders and Michael Phillips, "Arch-Os: An Operating System for Buildings," *Fabrication: Examining the Digital Practice of Architecture: Proceedings of the 23rd Annual Conference of the Association for*

*Computer Aided Design in Architecture and the 2004 Conference of the AIA Technology in Architectural Practice Knowledge Community,* ed. P. Beesley, Nancy Cheng, and R. S. Williamson (Cambridge and Toronto: University of Waterloo, Cambridge, and University of Toronto, 2004).

40. Operators of this latest generation of dockless bike-sharing systems are, among others, ofo bike, LimeBike, Reddy bike share, Mobike, and Spin.

41. Anne Bogart and Tina Landau, *The Viewpoints Book: A Practical Guide to Viewpoints and Composition* (New York: Theatre Communications Group, 2004).

42. From a conversation with the Viewpoints instructor and theater faculty member Jonathan Carr, 2016.

43. "Der Wert der Städte bestimmt sich nach der Zahl der Orte, die in ihnen, der Improvisation eingeräumt sind." Siegfried Kracauer, *Straßen in Berlin und anderswo* (Frankfurt: Suhrkamp, 2009), 71.

44. Graeme Gilloch, "Seen from the Window: Rhythm, Improvisation and the City," in *Bauhaus and the City: A Contested Heritage for a Challenging Future,* ed. Laura Colini and Frank Eckardt (Würzburg, Germany: Königshausen and Neumann, 2011), 201.

## 2. WHEN THE CITY BEGINS TO TALK

Epigraph: Paola Antonelli, "Talk to Me," accessed May 20, 2018, www.moma.org/interactives/exhibitions/2011/talktome. This quote is an excerpt from a longer text in the exhibition catalog Paola Antonelli, *Talk to Me: Design and the Communication Between People and Objects* (New York: Museum of Modern Art, 2011) from the exhibition *Talk to Me,* which took place at the Museum of Modern Art in New York, July 24–November 7, 2011.

1. Tibullus, *Elegies: Text, Introduction and Commentary,* ed. and trans. Robert Maltby (Cambridge, U.K.: Cairns, 2002), 2.5, 23.

2. William Mitchell in *City of Bits* had ample foresight when pondering, "Perhaps some electronic cartographer of the future will produce an appropriately nuanced Nolli map of the Net" (131). Not only would electronic cartographers map the Net, but electronic mapping would be folded back onto the city that Nolli once drew in ink.

3. Kevin Lynch, *The Image of the City* (Cambridge, Mass.: MIT Press, 1960), 2.

4. Lynch, *Image of the City,* 2.

5. Lynch, *Image of the City,* 2.

6. De Certeau, *Practice of Everyday Life,* 97.

7. De Certeau, *Practice of Everyday Life,* 93.

8. Mark Weiser, "The Computer for the 21st Century," *Scientific American* 265, no. 3 (1991): 94.

9. Manuel Castells, *The Rise of the Network Society* (Malden, Mass.: Wiley-Blackwell, 2010), 429.

10. Some of the more vigorous critiques of the smart city model can be found in Greenfield, *Against the Smart City;* and Hollands, "Critical Interventions."

11. William Mitchell, *Me++: The Cyborg Self and the Network City* (Cambridge, Mass.: MIT Press, 2003), 9.

12. Gilles Deleuze and Félix Guattari, *A Thousand Plateaus: Capitalism and Schizophrenia* (Minneapolis: University of Minnesota Press, 1987), 21.

13. Stefan Wray, "On Electronic Civil Disobedience," *Peace Review* 11, no. 1 (1999).

14. Castells, *Rise of the Network Society*, 408.

15. Castells, *Rise of the Network Society*, 77, 410.

16. Saskia Sassen, *The Global City: New York, London, Tokyo* (Princeton, N.J.: Princeton University Press, 1991).

17. Castells, *Rise of the Network Society*, 408.

18. Geoffrey Parker, Marshall Van Alstyne, and Sangeet Paul Choudary, *Platform Revolution: How Networked Markets Are Transforming the Economy and How to Make Them Work for You* (New York: Norton, 2016).

19. Catherine Soanes and Sara Hawker, *Compact Oxford English Dictionary of Current English* (Oxford: Oxford University Press, 2008), s.v. "real time."

20. Lewis Mumford, *Technics and Civilization* (Chicago: University of Chicago Press, 2010), 14.

21. Marshall McLuhan, *Understanding Media* (New York: Routledge, 2001).

22. Mumford, *Technics and Civilization*.

23. This discourse that juxtaposes the *virtual* with the *actual* is based on Gilles Deleuze, *Difference and Repetition* (London: Athlone, 1994); Lévy, *Becoming Virtual;* Tomás Maldonado, *Reale e virtuale* (Milan: Feltrinelli, 1998).

24. Pierre Lévy, *Il virtuale* (Milan: Raffaello Cortina Editore, 1997), 5–7.

25. Gilles Deleuze, *Bergsonism* (London: Zone Books, 1991), 42–43.

26. For an early approach to designing digitally augmented urban environments that looked for guidance to the type of place to articulate meaningful functionalities, see McCullough, *Digital Ground*.

27. A first step toward urban computing in a scenario described in Weiser, "Computer for the 21st Century," 102.

28. Mark Weiser and John Seely Brown, "The Coming Age of Calm Technology" (1996); Marcus Foth, *Handbook of Research on Urban Informatics: The Practice and Promise of the Real-Time City* (Hershey, Pa.: IGI Global, 2008); Adam Greenfield and Mark Shepard, *Urban Computing and Its Discontents* (New York: Architectural League of New York, 2007).

29. Some recent articles illustrate the issue of citizens and cities attempting to fight the effects of algorithm-based traffic routing through side streets with previously little road traffic by posting fake accident reports, inexistent speed bumps, and false rush-hour road blocks on navigation platforms to divert car routings: Alexis C. Madrigal, "The Perfect Selfishness of Mapping Apps," *Atlantic*, March 15, 2018; Steve Hendrix, "Traffic-Weary Homeowners and Waze Are at War, Again. Guess Who's Winning," *Washington Post*, June 5, 2016; Rick Paulas, "For the Good of Society—and Traffic!—Delete Your Map App," *New York*, December 11, 2017.

30. Batty, "Computable City."

31. The cities of Masdar and Songdo are striking examples of such green-field smart city planning and are discussed in Greenfield, *Against the Smart City*.

32. Hollands, "Beyond the Corporate Smart City?"

33. Kitchin, Lauriault, and McArdle, "Smart Cities."

34. Horst Rittel and Melvin Webber, "Dilemmas in a General Theory of Planning," *Policy Sciences* 4 (1973): 165.

35. Marvin, Luque-Ayala, and McFarlane, *Smart Urbanism*.

36. Datta, "Smart Entrepreneurial City," 52.

37. Odendaal, "Getting Smart."

38. Mitchell, *Me++*.

39. Amartya Sen, "Capability and Well-Being," in *The Quality of Life*, ed. Martha Nussbaum and Amartya Sen (Oxford: Oxford University Press, 1993), 31.

40. Nnaemeka, "Unexotic Underclass."

41. Neil Brenner and Christian Schmid, "Towards a New Epistemology of the Urban?" *City* 19, nos. 2–3 (2015); and the response in the same journal issue, Richard Walker, "Building a Better Theory of the Urban: A Response to 'Towards a New Epistemology of the Urban?'" *City* 19, nos. 2–3 (2015).

42. Taylor, *Moment of Complexity*, 106.

43. Roche et al., "Are 'Smart Cities' Smart Enough?"; Cardullo and Kitchin, "Being a 'Citizen' in the Smart City."

44. Townsend, *Smart Cities*, 284.

45. The argument for a nonanthropocentric design is outlined in Forlano, "Decentering the Human" (42) and is based on an earlier discussion in DiSalvo and Lukens, "Ropocentrism and the Nonhuman in Design."

46. Goldsmith and Crawford, *Responsive City*.

47. Hollands, "Will the Real Smart City Please Stand Up?"

48. Types of social currency are manifold, including "likes" from others to one's user profile and the visible display of the number of contributions or validation in the form of stars, hearts, or titles such as *mayor*.

49. An example for this kind of participation can be found in Kim, Mankoff, and Paulos, "Sensr"; Liu et al., "Going Beyond Citizen Data Collection."

50. Elinor Ostrom, "Crossing the Great Divide: Coproduction, Synergy, and Development," *World Development* 24, no. 6 (1996).

51. Hollands, "Beyond the Corporate Smart City?"

52. Eric Gordon and Stephen Walter, "Meaningful Inefficiencies: Resisting the Logic of Technological Efficiency in the Design of Civic Systems," in *Civic Media: Technology, Design, and Practice*, ed. Eric Gordon and Paul Mihailidis (Cambridge, Mass.: MIT Press, 2016).

53. Eric Gordon, "Meaningful Inefficiencies: Designing for Democratic Values in the Smart City," talk at ETH Zürich, May 3, 2018, accessed on YouTube, June 10, 2018, www.youtube.com/watch?v=sPognpWSk4U.

54. Notable are the pilot project Gratisstadrad, launched in Vienna in 2001, and the follow-up project Viennabike, launched in 2002. Both followed the example of Copenhagen's ByCyklen project, which was launched in 1995.

55. Charles Jencks and Nathan Silver, *Adhocism: The Case for Improvisation* (Cambridge, Mass.: MIT Press, 2013).

56. Jencks and Silver, *Adhocism*, viii.

57. Arthur Koestler, *The Act of Creation* (London: Pan Books, 1971).

58. Jeroen Beekmans and Joop de Boer, *Pop-Up City: City-Making in a Fluid World* (Amsterdam: BIS, 2014).

## 3. INTERFACE, INTERACT, IMPROVACT

Epigraph: Laurel, *Computers as Theatre*, 27.

1. The literature on interface design is extensive, and providing a full account goes beyond the scope of this book; a good critical introduction, written by one of the domain's key figures, is Kay, "User Interface."

2. An extensive discussion of the spatial concept of time can be found in Lewis Mumford, "Space, Distance, Movement," in *Technics and Civilization* (Chicago: University of Chicago Press, 2010).

3. McLuhan, *Understanding Media*, 167–68.

4. Clark and Brennan, "Grounding in Communication."

5. Clark and Brennan, "Grounding in Communication," 127.

6. Clark and Brennan, "Grounding in Communication," 128.

7. Monk, "Common Ground."

8. Dourish, *Where the Action Is*, 132–33.

9. Pask, *Conversation Theory*.

10. Pask, *Conversation Theory*.

11. Pask, "Architectural Relevance of Cybernetics," 496.

12. Erving Goffman, *The Presentation of Self in Everyday Life* (Garden City, N.Y.: Anchor Books, 1959), 15.

13. Lucy Suchman, "Making Work Visible," *Communications of the ACM* 38, no. 9 (1995).

14. Suchman, *Plans and Situated Actions*.

15. Don Norman, *The Design of Everyday Things: Revised and Expanded Edition* (New York: Basic Books, 2013), 43.

16. Dourish, *Where the Action Is*, 72.

17. Suchman, *Plans and Situated Actions*, viii.

18. Suchman, *Plans and Situated Actions*, viii.

19. Suchman, *Plans and Situated Actions*, ix.

20. A comprehensive introduction to activity theory can be found in Kaptelinin and Nardi, *Acting with Technology*.

21. Kaptelinin and Nardi, *Acting with Technology*.

22. Kaptelinin and Nardi, *Acting with Technology*, 256.

23. Don Ihde, *Technology and the Lifeworld: From Garden to Earth* (Bloomington: Indiana University Press, 1990).

24. Hans Achterhuis, *American Philosophy of Technology: The Empirical Turn* (Bloomington: Indiana University Press, 2001).

25. Peter-Paul Verbeek, "Beyond Interaction: A Short Introduction to Mediation Theory," *Interactions* 22, no. 3 (2015); Peter-Paul Verbeek, *What Things Do: Philosophical Reflections on Technology, Agency, and Design* (University Park: Penn State University Press, 2005).

26. Verbeek, "Beyond Interaction"; Verbeek, *What Things Do*; Don Ihde, *Postphenomenology and Technoscience: The Peking University Lectures* (Albany: SUNY Press, 2009).

27. Norman, foreword to Laurel, *Computers as Theatre*, xii.

28. Laurel, *Computers as Theatre*, 28.

29. Jeff Patton, "The New User Story Backlog Is a Map," October 8, 2008, https://jpattonassociates.com/the-new-backlog; Jeff Patton, "It's All in How You Slice," *Better Software*, January 2005.

30. James Kalbach, *Mapping Experiences: A Guide to Creating Value Through Journeys, Blueprints, and Diagrams* (Sebastopol, Calif.: O'Reilly, 2016).

31. Donna Lichaw, *The User's Journey: Storymapping Products That People Love* (Brooklyn, N.Y.: Rosenfeld Media, 2016).

32. Lichaw, *User's Journey*, 4.

33. Lichaw, *User's Journey*, 19.

34. Lichaw, *User's Journey*, xiii.

35. Arendt, *Human Condition*, 184.

36. De Certeau, *Practice of Everyday Life*, 93.

37. Arendt, *Human Condition*, 185–86.

38. Jonathon Colman, foreword to Lichaw, *User's Journey*, xii.

39. Arendt, *Human Condition*, 186.

40. Laurel, *Computers as Theatre*, 27.

41. Hans-Thies Lehmann, *Postdramatisches Theater* (Frankfurt: Verlag der Autoren, 1999); Hans-Thies Lehmann, *Postdramatic Theatre* (London: Routledge, 2006).

42. Erving Goffman, *Interaction Ritual: Essays in Face-to-Face Behavior* (New Brunswick, N.J.: Transaction, 2005), 144.

43. Peter Sloth Madsen and Michael Spencer, "Post-Dramatic Theatre in Design Research," Vimeo, uploaded July 12, 2015, vimeo.com/133277530.

44. Merja Ryöppy, Salu Ylirisku, Preben Friis, and Jacob Buur, "Postdramatic Theatre in Smart City Design," *Proceedings of the 20th International Academic Mindtrek Conference* (New York: Association for Computing Machinery, 2016).

45. Ryöppy et al., "Postdramatic Theatre," 463–64.

## 4. IMPROVISATION AS SYSTEM

Epigraph: Stephen Nachmanovitch, *Free Play: Improvisation in Life and Art* (New York: Tarcher/Putnam, 1991), 17.

1. Rudlin, *Commedia dell'Arte*, 14.

2. Massimo Troiani provided the first account of a performance in 1568; Mehnert, *Commedia dell'Arte*, 10.

3. Mehnert, *Commedia dell'Arte*.

4. Mehnert, *Commedia dell'Arte*, 30.

5. Justin Borrow, "Commedia dell'Arte: The Theatre of the Streets," Academia, 2014, www.academia.edu/15826213/Commedia_DellArte_The_Theatre_of_the_Streets; Mehnert, *Commedia dell'Arte*, 32.

6. Judith Chaffee and Oliver Crick, *The Routledge Companion to Commedia dell'Arte* (New York: Routledge, 2017).

7. Chaffee and Crick, *Routledge Companion to Commedia dell'Arte*, 233.

8. Arnold Aronson, *The Routledge Companion to Scenography* (New York: Routledge, 2017), 229.

9. Stanley Allan Sherman, "The Essential Scenario—Actors Freedom—Commedia dell'Arte," *Mask Arts Company Blog*, July 7, 2013, https://maskarts.com/wordpress/?p=468.

10. De Certeau, *Practice of Everyday Life*.

11. Derek Bailey, *Improvisation: Its Nature and Practice in Music* (New York: Da Capo, 1993).

12. Montuori, "Complexity of Improvisation."

13. Berliner, *Thinking in Jazz;* Weick, "Introductory Essay."

14. Immanuel Kant, *Critique of Judgment* (Indianapolis: Hackett, 1987), 181.

15. Jacques Derrida, "Psyche: Inventions of the Other," in *Reading de Man Reading*, ed. Lindsay Waters and Wlad Godzich (Minneapolis: University of Minnesota Press, 1989).

16. Landgraf, *Improvisation as Art*.

17. Berliner, *Thinking in Jazz;* Weick, "Introductory Essay."

18. Landgraf, *Improvisation as Art*, 36.

19. Montuori, "Complexity of Improvisation," 241.

20. Herbert Alexander Simon, *The Sciences of the Artificial* (Cambridge, Mass.: MIT Press, 1969); Taylor, *Moment of Complexity*.

21. Paul Berliner, quoting the drummer Max Roach, in *Thinking in Jazz*, 192.

22. Pask, "Architectural Relevance of Cybernetics," 495.

23. Arendt, *Human Condition*, 177.

24. Arendt, *Human Condition*, 178.

25. Peters, *Philosophy of Improvisation;* Martin Heidegger, "The Origin of the Work of Art," *Poetry, Language, Thought* 55 (1971).

26. Kent De Spain, *Landscape of the Now: A Topography of Movement Improvisation* (Oxford: Oxford University Press, 2014).

27. De Spain, *Landscape of the Now*, 114.

28. De Spain, *Landscape of the Now*, 116.

29. De Spain, *Landscape of the Now*, 116.

30. De Spain, *Landscape of the Now*, 116.

31. Bogart and Landau, *Viewpoints Book*.

32. De Spain, *Landscape of the Now*, 114.

33. De Spain, *Landscape of the Now*, 118.

34. Brian Walker, C. S. Holling, Stephen R. Carpenter, and Ann Kinzig, "Resilience, Adaptability and Transformability in Social-Ecological Systems," *Ecology and Society* 9, no. 2 (2004).

35. British Standards Institution, "Bs 65000:2014 Guidance on Organizational Resilience," accessed June 7, 2017, http://shop.bsigroup.com/ProductDetail/?pid=000000000030258792.

36. Bruno Latour, *Reassembling the Social: An Introduction to Actor-Network-Theory* (Oxford: Oxford University Press, 2005). A related but distinct perspective of agency in human-technology systems has been developed in the context of activity theory: Kaptelinin and Nardi, *Acting with Technology*.

37. Made by Italian company Ferrero since the 1970s and sold around the world, Kinder Surprise eggs appear to be banned from import in the United States because of the Federal Food, Drug, and Cosmetic Act, which prohibits confectionery products that contain a "non-nutritive object," unless the object has functional value. However, U.S. kids need not miss out on the surprises, as Ferrero is offering an alternative version of its Surprise eggs called Joy, in which only half the egg is chocolate while the other half makes up the toy.

38. Lehmann, *Postdramatic Theatre*, 143.

39. Lehmann, *Postdramatic Theatre*, 143.

40. Goffman, *Presentation of Self*.

41. Branko Kolarevic and Ali Malkawi, *Performative Architecture: Beyond Instrumentality* (New York: Routledge, 2005); Pedro Gadanho, "The Performative Turn," *Shrapnel Contemporary* (blog), February 24, 2012, https://shrapnelcontemporary.wordpress.com/2012/02/24/the-performative-turn.

42. Gillian Crampton Smith, "What Is Interaction Design?" in *Designing Interactions*, by Bill Moggridge (Cambridge, Mass.: MIT Press, 2007), xii.

43. Andrew Pickering, *The Cybernetic Brain: Sketches of Another Future* (Chicago: University of Chicago Press, 2011), 364.

44. From a lecture given by Constant Nieuwenhuys on November 7, 1963, at the Institute of Contemporary Arts in London, published in Constant Nieuwenhuys, "Lecture at the Institute of Contemporary Arts, London, 1963," in *Constant: New Babylon. To Us, Liberty* (Berlin: Hatje Cantz, 2016), 210.

45. Constant Nieuwenhuys, "Another City for Another Life, 1959," in *Constant: New Babylon*, 207.

46. Nieuwenhuys, "Lecture at the Institute of Contemporary Arts," 212.

47. Nieuwenhuys, "Another City for Another Life," 208.

48. John Ezard and Michael Billington, "Joan Littlewood," *Guardian*, September 23, 2002, quoted in Pickering, *Cybernetic Brain*, 365.

49. Usman Haque, "The Architectural Relevance of Gordon Pask," *Architectural Design* 77, no. 4 (2007): 56.

50. Haque, "Architectural Relevance of Gordon Pask," 56.

51. Pask, "Architectural Relevance of Cybernetics," 496.

52. Jordan Geiger, "Entr'acte, Interim, Interstice: Performing Publics and Media Across Scales of Time and Space," in *Entr'acte: Performing Publics, Pervasive Media, and Architecture*, ed. Jordan Geiger (New York: Palgrave Macmillan, 2015), 12.

53. Omar Khan, "Crowd Choreographies," in Geiger, *Entr'acte*, 134.

54. Elias Canetti, *Masse und Macht* (Frankfurt am Main: Fischer Taschenbuch, 1980).

55. Lehmann, *Postdramatic Theatre*, 143.

56. David P. Brown, *Noise Orders: Jazz, Improvisation, and Architecture* (Minneapolis: University of Minnesota Press, 2006); David P. Brown, "Lots Will Vary in the Available City," in *The Oxford Handbook of Critical Improvisation Studies*, vol. 2, ed. George E. Lewis and Benjamin Piekut (Oxford: Oxford University Press, 2016).

57. Brown, "Lots Will Vary," 66.

58. Christopher Dell and Ton Matton, "Improvisation Technology as Mode of Redesigning the Urban," in Lewis and Piekut, *Oxford Handbook of Critical Improvisation Studies*, 41.

59. Dietmar Offenhuber and Katja Schechtner, "Improstructure—An Improvisational Perspective on Smart Infrastructure Governance," *Cities* 72 (2018).

60. Simon Penny, "Improvisation and Interaction, Canons and Rules, Emergence and Play," in Lewis and Piekut, *Oxford Handbook of Critical Improvisation Studies*.

61. Omar Al Faleh, Nikolaos Chandolias, and Del Tredici Felix, "Towards an Integrated Design Process for Improvisational and Performative Interactive Environments," paper presented at the ACM Designing Interactive Systems 2014 Workshop: Human-Computer Improvisation, Vancouver, B.C., Canada, June 21–25, 2014.

## 5. AN IMPROVISATION-BASED MODEL FOR URBAN INTERACTION DESIGN

Epigraphs: Robert S. Boynton, "In 'Under the Sun,' a Documentary Masked and Unmasked," *New York Times,* July 1, 2016; Parker, Van Alstyne, and Choudary, *Platform Revolution,* 59; Mike Berardino, "Mike Tyson Explains One of His Most Famous Quotes," *Sun Sentinel,* November 9, 2012, www.sun-sentinel.com/sports/fl-xpm-2012-11-09-sfl-mike-tyson-explains-one-of-his-most-famous-quotes–20121109-story.html; Heinz von Foerster, "On Constructing a Reality," in *Understanding Understanding* (New York: Springer, 2003), 211; Philippe Petit, "The Journey Across the High Wire," TED2012 video, March 2, 2012, www.ted.com/talks/philippe_petit_the_journey_across_the_high_wire.

1. Peters, *Philosophy of Improvisation,* 12, referencing Niklas Luhmann.

2. Heidegger, "Origin of the Work of Art."

3. Arendt, *Human Condition.*

4. Arendt, *Human Condition,* 178.

5. Consider the recently established 311 public service centers and their real-time systems of interacting with citizens, or consider the numerous real-time public transport services accessible through smartphones and other connected devices.

6. Umberto Eco, *The Open Work* (Cambridge, Mass.: Harvard University Press, 1989).

7. Eco, *Open Work,* 15.

8. Khan, "Crowd Choreographies."

9. Eco, *Open Work,* 20.

10. Brown, "Lots Will Vary."

11. Eco, *Open Work,* 15.

12. Examples of dockless bike-sharing systems are those operated by ofo and LimeBike, operative in numerous cities around the globe.

13. Suchman, *Plans and Situated Actions.*

14. Dell and Matton, "Improvisation Technology," 40.

15. Lehmann, *Postdramatic Theatre*, 142.

16. For an in-depth discussion of aspects of time and timing in Action Theater improvisation, see Ruth Zaporah, *Action Theater: The Improvisation of Presence* (Berkeley, Calif.: North Atlantic Books, 1995), 9. Zaporah is the founder of Action Theater.

17. Eric Charles White, *Kaironomia: On the Will-to-Invent* (Ithaca, N.Y.: Cornell University Press, 1987), 3.

18. My understanding of karate and its underlying principles is based on several years of practice with Sensei Davide Rizzo in Venice, Italy, and with the Japan Karate Association of Boston, as well as from texts such as Kenji Tokitsu, *The Inner Art of Karate: Cultivating the Budo Spirit in Your Practice*, trans. Sherab Chödzin Kohn (Boston: Shambhala, 2012); and Gichin Funakoshi, *Karate-Do Kyohan: The Master Text* (Tokyo: Kodansha International, 2013).

19. Henri Lefebvre, *Rhythmanalysis: Space, Time, and Everyday Life* (London: Continuum, 2004), 68.

20. Henri Lefebvre, *The Production of Space* (Oxford, U.K.: Blackwell, 1991).

21. Lefebvre, *Rhythmanalysis*, viii.

22. Lefebvre, *Rhythmanalysis*, 8.

23. Lefebvre, *Rhythmanalysis*, 7.

24. Lefebvre, *Rhythmanalysis*, 6.

25. White, *Kaironomia*.

26. An account can be found in John Thackara, *In the Bubble: Designing in a Complex World* (Cambridge, Mass.: MIT Press, 2006), 46.

27. Goffman, *Presentation of Self*, 2.

28. The language of "observable and reportable" is from Harold Garfinkel, *Studies in Ethnomethodology* (Englewood Cliffs, N.J.: Prentice-Hall, 1967), 1–2, quoted in Dourish, *Where the Action Is*, 79.

29. Goffman, *Presentation of Self*, 3, quoting William Isaac Thomas, *Social Behavior and Personality* (New York: Social Science Research Council, 1951), 93.

30. Goffman, *Presentation of Self*, 6.

31. A seminal discussion on the center and periphery of attention in the context of interaction design can be found in Weiser and Brown, "Coming Age."

32. Greg Corness and Thecla Schiphorst, "Performing with a System's Intention: Embodied Cues in Performer-System Interaction," *Proceedings of the 9th ACM Conference on Creativity & Cognition*, ed. Ellen Yi-Luen Do, Steven Dow, Jack Ox, Steve Smith, Kazushi Nishimoto, and Chek Tien Tan (New York: ACM, 2013).

33. David Sirkin, Brian Mok, Stephen Yang, and Wendy Ju, "Mechanical Ottoman: How Robotic Furniture Offers and Withdraws Sup-

port," *Proceedings of the Tenth Annual ACM/IEEE International Conference on Human-Robot Interaction* (New York: ACM, 2015).

34. Harold Garfinkel, *Studies in Ethnomethodology* (Englewood Cliffs, N.J.: Prentice-Hall, 1967), 1–2.

35. Dourish, *Where the Action Is*, 80.

36. Dourish, *Where the Action Is*, 80.

37. Suchman, *Plans and Situated Actions*, 52.

38. Suchman, *Plans and Situated Actions*, 52.

39. Donella H. Meadows, *Thinking in Systems: A Primer* (White River Junction, Vt.: Chelsea Green, 2008).

40. Thackara, *In the Bubble*, 6; Moritz Stefaner, "Process and Progress: A Practitioner's Perspective on the How, What and Why of Data Visualization New Challenges for Data Design," in *New Challenges for Data Design*, ed. David Bihanic (London: Springer, 2015); Paolo Ciuccarelli, M. I. Sessa, and Maurizio Tucci, "CoDe: A Graphic Language for Complex System Visualization," *Proceedings of the Italian Association for Information Systems (ItAIS)* (2010); Katy Börner, "Plug-and-Play Macroscopes," *Communications of the ACM* 54, no. 3 (2011).

41. Joël de Rosnay, *The Macroscope: A New World Scientific System* (New York: Harper and Row, 1979), xiii.

42. Rittel and Webber, "Dilemmas in a General Theory."

43. William Cronon, "The Trouble with Wilderness: A Response," *Environmental History* 1 (1996).

44. Peter Handke, *Kaspar and Other Plays* (New York: Macmillan, 1989).

45. Jonathan Massey and Brett Snyder, "Occupying Wall Street: Places and Spaces of Political Action," *Places Journal*, September 2012; Jonathan Massey and Brett Snyder, "The Hypercity That Occupy Built," in Geiger, *Entr'acte*.

46. Patrick Kingsley, "People Smugglers Using Facebook to Lure Migrants into 'Italy Trips,' " *Guardian*, May 8, 2015, www.theguardian.com/world/2015/may/08/people-smugglers-using-facebook-to-lure-migrants-into-italy-trips; Patrick Kinsley, "Libya's People Smugglers: Inside the Trade That Sells Refugees Hopes of a Better Life," *Guardian*, April 24, 2015, www.theguardian.com/world/2015/apr/24/libyas-people-smugglers-how-will-they-catch-us-theyll-soon-move-on.

47. On June 11, 2018, the NGO ship *Aquarius* carrying 629 illegal migrants saved from the Mediterranean Sea was denied entry to ports in Malta and Italy as their governments blocked access to their ports. The ship later headed to Valencia, Spain.

48. Gabrys, *Program Earth*.

49. Isabelle Stengers, "The Cosmopolitical Proposal," in *Making Things Public: Atmospheres of Democracy*, ed. Bruno Latour and Peter Weibel (Karisruhe, Germany: ZKM / Center for Art and Media, 2005).

## 6. EXPERIMENTATION WITH UNCERTAINTY
## AND THE UNPREDICTABLE

Epigraph: Zaporah, *Action Theater*, 24.

1. A very thorough account of the evolution of bike-sharing systems around the world can be found in Susan Shaheen, Stacey Guzman, and Hua Zhang, "Bikesharing in Europe, the Americas, and Asia: Past, Present, and Future," *Transportation Research Record: Journal of the Transportation Research Board* 2143 (2010). Given the date of publication of that text, the account stops short of the currently emerging dockless bike-sharing systems.

2. The dynamism of this emergent business is illustrated by the fact that during the writing and production of this book, ofo bike sharing not only entered the U.S. market and spread across several cities but also concluded U.S. operations entirely again in the summer of 2018.

3. oBike, "FAQs," accessed February 25, 2019, www.o.bike/au/faqs.

4. Adam Vaccaro, "Thousands of Dockless Bikes Headed for Boston's Suburbs," *Boston Globe*, April 13, 2018, www.bostonglobe.com/metro/2018/04/13/thousands-dockless-bikes-are-headed-for-boston-suburbs/ugXMAudzAhtHvXloZ6jeBJ/story.html.

5. An account of balancing strategies in dockless bike-sharing systems can be found in Ling Pan, Qingpeng Cai, Zhixuan Fang, Pingzhong Tang, and Longbo Huang, "Rebalancing Dockless Bike Sharing Systems," arXiv preprint, arXiv:1802.04592 (2018).

6. For accounts of bikes parked on trees and on rail tracks in Vienna, see Leserreporter, "Fotos: Diese Ofo-Bikes Parken Einfach Überall," *Heute*, November 4, 2017, www.heute.at/community/leser/story/Fotos-Diese-Ofo-Bikes-parken-einfach-ueberall-53861254; Leserreporter, "Unbekannte Werfen Ofo-Bikes Auf U4-Gleise," *Heute*, April 29, 2018, www.heute.at/community/leser/story/Unbekannte-werfen-Ofo-Bikes-auf-U4-Gleise-42450583.

7. Stengers, "Cosmopolitical Proposal."

8. Benjamin Schneider, "How Park(ing) Day Went Global," CityLab, September 15, 2017, www.citylab.com/life/2017/09/from-parking-to-parklet/539952.

9. Liza Pratt, *Divisadero Trail Parklet Impact Report* (San Francisco: San Francisco Great Streets Project, 2010); Erin Rice and Andrew Ehrich, *17th Street Trial Plaza User and Perception Analysis* (San Francisco: San Francisco Great Streets Project, 2009).

10. Detailed information about the Pavement to Parks program can be found on the program's online site, http://pavementtoparks.org. I was helped in understanding the parklet system and process by a case study developed by my student Joshua Friedman as part of the Design Tactics

and Operations course I taught at Northeastern University's School of Architecture in spring 2017.

11. Vincent Agoe, Rennie Newton, and Alexandra Stein, *The Public Perception of San Francisco's Parklets: Divisadero Cluster* (San Francisco: San Francisco Great Streets Project, 2014); Alison Ecker and Stella Kim, *Are Parklets Public? Perceptions of Polk Street Parklets* (Berkeley: University of California, Berkeley, College of Environmental Design Research Methods in Environmental Design, 2014).

12. Besides the project information available on the HQ Architects website, additional information was gathered during a phone interview with the studio's founder, Erez Ella, on June 5, 2018.

13. HQ Architects, "Warde, Dynamic Street Installation, Jerusalem," accessed May 20, 2018, www.hqa.co.il/mies_portfolio/warde.

14. Anders and Phillips, "Arch-Os," 289.

## 7. IMPROVISATION AS TECHNIQUE AND PRACTICE FOR DESIGN

Epigraph: Koestler, *The Act of Creation*, 120.

1. Kari Kuutti, Giulio Iacucci, and Carlo Iacucci, "Acting to Know: Improving Creativity in the Design of Mobile Services by Using Performances," *Proceedings of the 4th Conference on Creativity & Cognition* (New York: ACM, 2002); Marion Buchenau and Jane Fulton Suri, "Experience Prototyping," *Proceedings of the 3rd Conference on Designing Interactive Systems: Processes, Practices, Methods, and Techniques* (New York: ACM, 2000).

2. Eva Brandt and Camilla Grunnet, "Evoking the Future: Drama and Props in User Centered Design," *Proceedings of the 6th Participatory Design Conference (PDC 2000)*, ed. T. Cherkasky, J. Greenbaum, P. Mambrey, and J. K. Pors (Palo Alto, Calif.: CPSR, 2000).

3. Bill Gaver, Tony Dunne, and Elena Pacenti, "Design: Cultural Probes," *Interactions* 6, no. 1 (1999).

4. Elizabeth Gerber, "Improvisation Principles and Techniques for Design," *Proceedings of the SIGCHI Conference on Human Factors in Computing Systems* (New York: ACM, 2007); Elizabeth Gerber, "Using Improvisation to Enhance the Effectiveness of Brainstorming," *Proceedings of the SIGCHI Conference on Human Factors in Computing Systems* (New York: ACM, 2009).

5. A good introduction to movement improvisation in the form of interviews with several of its most prominent performers and founders can be found in De Spain, *Landscape of the Now*.

6. De Certeau, *Practice of Everyday Life*, 97, quoting Christopher Alexander, *A City Is Not a Tree*.

7. Bogart and Landau, *Viewpoints Book*, 7.

8. Bogart and Landau, *Viewpoints Book*, 19.

9. One of the few written documents on Viewpoints is the excellent account by Bogart and Landau, *Viewpoints Book*. My understanding of Viewpoints is based mainly on that book, from observing Viewpoints practice sessions, and from conversations with Jonathan Carr, a theater director and professor who has trained with the Viewpoints founder, Anne Bogart.

10. Bogart and Landau, *Viewpoints Book*, 43.

11. A recent project in the city of Copenhagen offers one example of a prototype. See Diane Cardwell, "Copenhagen Lighting the Way to Greener, More Efficient Cities," *New York Times*, December 9, 2014, www.nytimes.com/2014/12/09/business/energy-environment/copenhagen-lighting-the-way-to-greener-more-efficient-cities.html.

12. This apparent movement was defined as *phi phenomenon* in 1910 by Max Wertheimer, cofounder of Gestalt psychology. D. Brett King, William Douglas Woody, and Wayne Viney, *A History of Psychology: Ideas and Context*, 5th ed. (New York: Pearson, 2013), 374.

13. This refers to chapter 7 of de Certeau's *Practice of Everyday Life*, which is part of the book's section on spatial practices.

14. Dell and Matton, "Improvisation Technology," 50.

15. Lacaton and Vassal, in Andreas Ruby and Ilka Ruby, *Urban Transformation* (Berlin: Ruby, 2008), 254, quoted in Dell and Matton, "Improvisation Technology," 50.

16. Dell and Matton, "Improvisation Technology," 50.

17. Brown, *Noise Orders*; Brown, "Lots Will Vary."

18. Notably, in 1994, Apple sued Microsoft alleging the illegal copying of Macintosh's "look and feel" in Windows.

## 8. EPILOGUE

Epigraph: Philippe Petit, *Creativity: The Perfect Crime* (New York: Riverhead Books, 2014), 127.

1. The quote appears to be based on the old Yiddish proverb "Der mensch tracht, ün Got lacht" (Man plans and God laughs). Ignaz Bernstein, *Jüdische Sprichwörter und Redensarten* (Frankfurt am Main: Kauffmann, 1908), 166.

2. Petit, *Creativity*; Koestler, *Act of Creation*.

3. Suchman, *Plans and Situated Actions*.

4. Arendt, *Human Condition*.

# INDEX